CURTAI

CURTAIN CALL
101 Portraits in Verse

edited by
HUGO WILLIAMS

faber and faber

First published in 2001
by Faber and Faber Limited
3 Queen Square London WC1N 3AU

Photoset by Wilmaset Ltd, Birkenhead, Wirral
Printed in Italy

The right of Hugo Williams to be identified as editor of this work
has been asserted in accordance with Section 77 of the Copyright,
Designs and Patents Act 1988

A CIP record for this book
is available from the British Library

ISBN 0–571–20723–5

2 4 6 8 10 9 7 5 3 1

Contents

Introduction ix

Who's Who W. H. AUDEN 3
Mythology LAWRENCE DURRELL 4
My Mother ROBERT MEZEY 5
Complaint IAN HAMILTON 7
Message HAROLD PINTER 8
One Man One Vote PATRICIA BEER 9
Mary Bly JAMES WRIGHT 10
By Candlelight SYLVIA PLATH 11
The Beach TED HUGHES 13
The Picture of Little T. C. in a Prospect of Flowers
    ANDREW MARVELL 16
From a Childhood RAINER MARIA RILKE 18
To My Brother Miguel CÉSAR VALLEJO 19
The Little Brother JAMES REEVES 20
Bells for John Whiteside's Daughter JOHN CROWE
    RANSOM 21
The Boy Actor NOËL COWARD 22
Elvis Presley THOM GUNN 25
My Cat, Jeoffrey CHRISTOPHER SMART 26
And now the house-dog stretched once more EMILY
    BRONTË 30
Winter: My Secret CHRISTINA ROSSETTI 32
The Ballad of Villon and Fat Madge FRANÇOIS VILLON 34
Epistle to Miss Blount, on Her Leaving the Town, after the
    Coronation ALEXANDER POPE 36
A Beautiful Young Nymph Going to Bed JONATHAN
    SWIFT 38
Mews Flat Mona WILLIAM PLOMER 41

Do Take Muriel Out STEVIE SMITH 44
Sun and Fun JOHN BETJEMAN 45
Friedrich CHARLES CAUSLEY 46
Alfred Corning Clark ROBERT LOWELL 48
Fleming Helphenstine E. A. ROBINSON 50
Aspects of Robinson WELDON KEES 51
Paysage Triste T. S. ELIOT 52
The Farmer's Bride CHARLOTTE MEW 53
Margery Kempe ELIZABETH SMART 55
A Nun Takes the Veil BERNARD O'DONOGHUE 56
'Absolon' from The Miller's Tale GEOFFREY CHAUCER 58
The Description of Sir Geoffrey Chaucer ROBERT
    GREENE 60
from Livings PHILIP LARKIN 61
from This is Your Subject Speaking ANDREW MOTION 62
Why Brownlee Left PAUL MULDOON 64
Butch Weldy EDGAR LEE MASTERS 65
House Guest ELIZABETH BISHOP 66
Cinquevalli EDWIN MORGAN 69
Of Ane Blak-Moir WILLIAM DUNBAR 72
Resolution and Independence WILLIAM
    WORDSWORTH 74
An Old Man's Winter Night ROBERT FROST 79
The Fisherman W. B. YEATS 80
Casualty SEAMUS HEANEY 82
The Gap in the Hedge R. S. THOMAS 86
David Garrick OLIVER GOLDSMITH 87
In Church THOMAS HARDY 89
You Don't Know What Love Is RAYMOND CARVER 90
birthday party CHARLES BUKOWSKI 95
I Love Drunks FAY HART 97
The Talented Man WINTHROP MACKWORTH PRAED 99
The mixer LOUIS MACNEICE 102

Rastignac at 45 THOM GUNN 103
'I was in the Forum once at a loose end' CATULLUS 105
The Great War Major ALAN ROSS 107
The Stalin Epigram OSIP MANDELSTAM 109
Epitaph on a Tyrant W. H. AUDEN 110
Dead Soldiers JAMES FENTON 111
Ali Ben Shufti ANTHONY THWAITE 114
Behaviour of Fish in an Egyptian Tea Garden KEITH
    DOUGLAS 116
Egyptian Dancer at Shubra BERNARD SPENCER 118
Dreaming in the Shanghai Restaurant D. J. ENRIGHT 119
Caravaggio: Self-Portrait with Severed Head ALAN
    JENKINS 120
To maystres Margaret Hussey JOHN SKELTON 122
The Vicar of Bray ANONYMOUS 124
By the Statue of King Charles at Charing Cross LIONEL
    JOHNSON 126
A Satyr on Charles II JOHN WILMOT, EARL OF
    ROCHESTER 128
[Character of George Villiers, Duke of Buckingham] from
    Absolom and Achitophel JOHN DRYDEN 130
The Duke of Buckingham ALEXANDER POPE 131
How pleasant to know Mr Lear EDWARD LEAR 132
Edward Lear W. H. AUDEN 134
Aunt Helen T. S. ELIOT 135
Elegy THEODORE ROETHKE 136
The Late Richard Dadd, 1817–1886 MICHAEL
    HOFMANN 137
Hard Rock Returns to Prison from the Hospital for the
    Criminal Insane ETHERIDGE KNIGHT 139
from Peter Grimes GEORGE CRABBE 141
The Ephemeral Past ANTONIO MACHADO 143
Next Day RANDALL JARRELL 145

You are Old, Father William LEWIS CARROLL 148

A Song of a Young Lady to Her Ancient Lover JOHN
    WILMOT, EARL OF ROCHESTER 150

An Old Man C. P. CAVAFY 151

To an Old Lady WILLIAM EMPSON 152

Wellingtonia STEPHEN ROMER 153

Uncle Stan CHARLES CAUSLEY 155

To Eugene Lambe in Heaven DEREK MAHON 157

Danny J. M. SYNGE 160

How M'Ginnis Went Missing A. B. (BANJO)
    PATERSON 162

Tommy RUDYARD KIPLING 164

An Elegy DAVID GASCOYNE 166

Waring ROBERT BROWNING 169

The Ballad of Lord Timbal JOHN FULLER 178

Suicide LOUIS MACNEICE 183

An Epitaph on M. H. CHARLES COTTON 184

On the Death of Dr Robert Levet SAMUEL JOHNSON 186

On the Death of Mr William Harvey ABRAHAM
    COWLEY 188

The Unknown Citizen W. H. AUDEN 190

The Self-Unseeing THOMAS HARDY 192

The Old Station at Cahors VALÉRY LARBAUD 193

Now Read On NEIL RENNIE 194

Acknowledgements 195

Index of Poets 199

Index of First Lines 202

Introduction

The last anthology I edited was in 1956, when I was fourteen. My sister had gained prestige by making one for my
father the previous Christmas and I was eager to reap the
same favour. 'Anthology' – the technical-sounding word,
like some weird branch of science, would bestow authority
on what was really just a notebook with poems copied into
it.

I got the book back, like a piece of homework, when my
father died. Opening it again, I marvelled at the handwrit-
ing and taste in poetry striving so hard to mimic his own –
Shakespeare and Milton standing equal in my eyes with
Henley, Flecker, Chesterton, Brooke, Masefield, Omar
Khayyam, Carla Lanyon Lanyon and Margaret Willy. The
effort of neatness, over a hundred pages, was painful to
behold, but I looked with envy and nostalgia at the excited
'Turn quickly' I wrote at the bottom of a page on which I
was copying out Laurie Lee's 'Town Owl'. I would be happy
if anyone felt inclined to turn the page quickly while reading any of the poems here.

My problem, as I remember it, was not quality of poetry so
much as quantity. I soon used up all the poems I knew and
had to resort to copying in my own pastiche versions,
mostly of Edward Fitzgerald and Arthur Waley, to fill up
the blank pages (which is how I first got interested in the
subject). The anthology is intriguing to me now as a snap-
shot of my untutored search for modern poetry – even if it
does give pride of place to John Wain and Laurie Lee (perhaps they are due for re-assessment). My copying out finally
breasted the tape with Vernon Scannell's 'The Unsuccessful

Poet' (no irony intended) and my father was duly touched by my slightly illegible Christmas present.

I got it out again recently to see if I could learn anything from my youthful effort. As before, my problem was not quality so much as quantity: this time how to thin down the multitudes. Gradually, I learnt the anthologist's art of gathering in with one hand while chucking out with the other. As I started the unfamiliar task of reading through the great collected works, I saw that the person poem, the character sketch, had always been with us, from Chaucer and Skelton through Goldsmith and Wordsworth to Frost, Auden and MacNeice, with an increase in quantity in the modern period. My initial list contained twelve poets with more than one poem to their name: Auden, Durrell, Hughes, Gunn, MacNeice, Catullus, Beer, Ransom, Pope, Causley, Cavafy, Hofmann and Eliot.

I started out with a poem I later realized I had copied into my old notebook anthology: 'Character of George Villiers, Duke of Buckingham' by John Dryden, which, along with the poems in Robert Lowell's *Life Studies*, I came to think of as a touchstone of excellence in the genre. It also happened to be the only poem on my list I had had to learn by heart. I remember a Mr Somebody telling us what 'epitome' meant and he must have been good, because I got it first time:

> A man so various, that he seemed to be
> Not one, but all mankind's epitome.
> Stiff in opinions, always in the wrong;
> Was everything by starts, and nothing long:
> But, in the course of one revolving moon,
> Was chemist, fiddler, statesman and buffoon;

Everyone likes the poem because they recognize someone they know, or, more likely, themselves. In my own case, it was my father who played the part of George Villiers:

> Railing and praising were his usual themes;
> And both (to show his judgement) in extremes:
> So over violent, or over civil,
> That every man, with him, was God or Devil.

One phrase in particular – 'Stiff in opinions, always in the wrong' – clung to my perception of my father. It wasn't until long after I had unconsciously plagiarized the line for a poem about him – 'imperious, categorical, always in the wrong / *and rightly so*' – that I realized where it had come from.

A verse portrait differs from other poems in that the performance is a sort of collaboration; the subject may not be sitting there, he is nevertheless exerting an influence on the work. This means that a poem like Robert Mezey's 'My Mother', though satirical, cannot help but express affection, whereas the reverse may be true of Lowell's seemingly admiring sketch of the reptilian rich man Alfred Corning Clark.

If Dryden's Buckingham was the original inspiration for my gallery of characters, later enthusiasms for Thom Gunn and Robert Lowell had a more far-reaching influence. Gunn's 'Elvis Presley' (which gave us 'revolt into style') isn't his greatest poem, but it does have a talismanic quality as the poem which first brought it home to me that poetry was still being written in the modern age. Robert Lowell's *Life Studies* was a book that changed the way we look at the past and led the way into the age of biography. With his example in mind, I found it possible to look through the back catalogue and pull out many 'life studies' that might not otherwise have seemed so obvious.

Anthology-making is paper intensive: instead of reading things, you photocopy vast numbers of poems and put them in efficient-seeming folders. Tension builds with impossible choices: Betjeman versus Cavafy, Coward versus Sitwell. Do you go for the great performances, Ulysses, Felix Randal, Ozymandias, or the interesting revivals, Edgar Lee Masters's 'Butch Weldy', William Plomer's 'Mews Flat Mona', which reflect better on your research?

Running order is the anthologist's holy grail. This is where he gets to display his brilliance with suggestive or ironical juxtapositions. My idea was to create a great daisy chain of poems, with every one casting an eye both forward and back; a virtually impossible task. I soon discovered that you cannot do this in your head, or even on paper. You need a large room, with, ideally, a great many chairs in it to put the poems on. You then stand in the middle with wildly staring eyes and attempt to conduct the storm. After many hours and many strong cups of coffee, it came to me in a flash that it didn't matter what order they were in because everything is connected to everything else anyway.

CURTAIN CALL

Who's Who

A shilling life will give you all the facts:
How Father beat him, how he ran away,
What were the struggles of his youth, what acts
Made him the greatest figure of his day:
Of how he fought, fished, hunted, worked all night,
Though giddy, climbed new mountains; named a sea:
Some of the last researchers even write
Love made him weep his pints like you and me.

With all his honours on, he sighed for one
Who, say astonished critics, lived at home;
Did little jobs about the house with skill
And nothing else; could whistle; would sit still
Or potter round the garden; answered some
Of his long marvellous letters but kept none.

Mythology

All my favourite characters have been
Out of all pattern and proportion:
Some living in villas by railways,
Some like Katsimbalis heard but seldom seen,
And others in banks whose sunless hands
Moved like great rats on ledgers.

Tibble, Gondril, Purvis, the Duke of Puke,
Shatterblossom and Dude Bowdler
Who swelled up in Jaffa and became a tree:
Hollis who had wives killed under him like horses
And that man of destiny,
Ramon de Something who gave lectures
From an elephant founded a society
To protect the inanimate against cruelty.
He gave asylum to aged chairs in his home,
Lampposts and crockery, everything that
Seemed to him suffering he took in
Without mockery.

The poetry was in the pity. No judgment
Disturbs people like these in their frames
O men of the Marmion class, sons of the free.

ROBERT MEZEY

My Mother

My mother writes from Trenton,
a comedian to the bone
but underneath, serious
and all heart. 'Honey,' she says,
'be a mensch and Mary too,
its no good to worry, you
are doing the best you can
your Dad and everyone
thinks you turned out very well
as long as you pay your bills
nobody can say a word
you can tell them to drop dead
so save a dollar it can't
hurt – remember Frank you went
to highschool with? he still lives
with his wife's mother, his wife
works while he writes his books and
did he ever sell a one
the four kids run around naked
36 and he's never had,
you'll forgive my expression
even a pot to piss in
or a window to throw it,
such a smart boy he couldnt
read the footprints on the wall
honey you think you know all
the answers you dont, please try
to put some money away
believe me it wouldn't hurt

artist shmartist life's too short
for that kind of, forgive me,
horseshit, I know what you want
better than you, all that counts
is to make a good living
and the best of everything,
as Sholem Aleichem said
he was a great writer did
you ever read his books dear,
you should make what he makes a year
anyway he says some place
Poverty is no disgrace
but its no honor either
that's what I say,
                    love,
                        Mother'

Complaint

I've done what I could. My boys run wild now.
They seek their chances while their mother rots here.
And up the road, the man,
My one man, who touched me everywhere,
Falls to bits under the ground.

I am dumpy, obtuse, old and out of it.
At night, I can feel my hands prowl over me,
Lightly probing at my breasts, my knees,
The folds of my belly,
Now and then pressing and sometimes,
In their hunger, tearing me.
I live alone.

My boys run, leaving their mother as they would a stone
That rolls on in the playground after the bell has gone.
I gather dust and I could almost love the grave.
To have small beasts room in me would be something.
But here, at eight again, I watch the blossoms break
Beyond this gravel yard.
I know how to behave.

Message

Jill. Fred phoned. He can't make tonight.
He said he'd call again, as soon as poss.
I said (on your behalf) OK, no sweat.
He said to tell you he was fine,
Only the crap, he said, you know, it sticks,
The crap you have to fight.
You're sometimes nothing but a walking shithouse.

I was well acquainted with the pong myself,
I told him, and I counselled calm.
Don't let the fuckers get you down,
Take the lid off the kettle a couple of minutes,
Go on the town, burn someone to death,
Find another tart, give her some hammer,
Live while you're young, until it palls,
Kick the first blind man you meet in the balls.

Anyway he'll call again.

I'll be back in time for tea.

Your loving mother.

PATRICIA BEER

One Man One Vote

My railwayman father voted
Only once in his entire life.
Politics was for the children
Of this present world and not for
Those who were marching to Zion.

He would not even vote Tory
Though he knew they had the breeding
And wealth that could help you, and though
The local candidate's daughter
Had by chance the same name as me.

Yet at sixty-three he went out
One evening, furtive after dark
But swashbuckling, down to the polls
To vote for a man who once worked
On the railways: a guard, Father thought.

Mary Bly

I sit here, doing nothing, alone, worn out by long winter.
I feel the light breath of the newborn child.
Her face is smooth as the side of an apricot,
Eyes quick as her blond mother's hands.
She has full, soft, red hair, and as she lies quiet
In her tall mother's arms, her delicate hands
Weave back and forth.
I feel the seasons changing beneath me,
Under the floor.
She is braiding the waters of air into the plaited manes
Of happy colts.
They canter, without making a sound, along the shores
Of melting snow.

By Candlelight

This is winter, this is night, small love—
A sort of black horsehair,
A rough, dumb country stuff
Steeled with the sheen
Of what green stars can make it to our gate.
I hold you on my arm.
It is very late.
The dull bells tongue the hour.
The mirror floats us at one candle power.

This is the fluid in which we meet each other,
This haloey radiance that seems to breathe
And lets our shadows wither
Only to blow
Them huge again, violent giants on the wall.
One match scratch makes you real.
At first the candle will not bloom at all—
It snuffs its bud
To almost nothing, to a dull blue dud.

I hold my breath until you creak to life,
Balled hedgehog,
Small and cross. The yellow knife
Grows tall. You clutch your bars.
My singing makes you roar.
I rock you like a boat
Across the Indian carpet, the cold floor,
While the brass man
Kneels, back bent, as best he can

Hefting his white pillar with the light
That keeps the sky at bay,
The sack of black! It is everywhere, tight, tight!
He is yours, the little brassy Atlas—
Poor heirloom, all you have,
At his heels a pile of five brass cannonballs,
No child, no wife.
Five balls! Five bright brass balls!
To juggle with, my love, when the sky falls.

The Beach

You lashed for release, like a migrant eel in November.
You needed the sea. I knew not much more
About Westcountry beaches than you did.
We are surrounded, I said, by magnificent beaches.
You'd seen the cliffs – a slashed and tilted gorge
Near Hartland, where we'd picked blackberries
That first somnambulist week of your ecstasy
With your brother. But now you needed a beach
Like your drug. Your undertow withdrawal
Blinded and choked you. It darkened a darkness darker.
England was so filthy! Only the sea
Could scour it. Your ocean salts would scour you.
You wanted to be washed, scoured, sunned.
That 'jewel in the head' – your flashing thunderclap miles
Of Nauset surf. The slew of horse-shoe crabs
And sand-dollars. You craved like oxygen
American earlier summers, yourself burnt dark –
Some prophecy mislaid, somehow. England
Was so poor! Was black paint cheaper? Why
Were English cars all black – to hide the filth?
Or to stay respectable, like bowlers
And umbrellas? Every vehicle a hearse.
The traffic procession a hushing leftover
Of Victoria's perpetual funeral Sunday –
The funeral of colour and light and life!
London a morgue of dinge – English dinge.
Our sole indigenous art-form – depressionist!
And why were everybody's
Garments so deliberately begrimed?

Grubby-looking, like a camouflage? 'Alas!
We have never recovered,' I said, 'from our fox-holes,
Our trenches, our fatigues and our bomb-shelters.

But I remembered my shock of first sighting
The revolving edge of Manhattan
From the deck of the *Queen Elizabeth* –
That merry-go-round palette of American cars.
Everywhere the big flower of freedom!
The humming-bird of light at the retina!
Then the weird shameful pain of uncrumpling
From wartime hibernation, cramped, unshucking
My utility habit – deprivation
Worn with the stupid pride of a demob outfit,
A convalescence not quite back into the world.

Now I wanted to show you such a beach
Would set inside your head another jewel,
And lift you like the gentlest electric shock
Into an altogether other England –
An Avalon for which I had the wavelength,
Deep inside my head a little crystal.

For some reason I'd fixed on Woolacombe Sands.
I had seen that mile of surf in its haze
But only across the bay from Baggy headland
Where the peregrine went over and the shark under,
And the seal came in, and the sea-flash
Was gathered and crimped, tucked and crewelled
Into needlework by the cliff-top flora –
A brilliant original for Hilliard's miniatures.

Your crisis came late in the day. It was dusk when we got there
After a steamed-up hour of November downpour
And black cars sploshing through pot-hole puddles.

The rain had stopped. Three or four other cars
Waited for walkers – distant and wrapped in their dowds.
A car-park streetlamp made the whole scene hopeless.
The sea moved near, stunned after the rain.
Unperforming. Above it
The blue-black heap of the West collapsed slowly,
Comfortless as a cold iron stove
Standing among dead cinders
In some roofless ruin. You refused to get out.
You sat behind your mask, inaccessible –
Staring towards the ocean that had failed you.
I walked to the water's edge. A dull wave
Managed to lift and flop. Then a weak hiss
Rolled black oil-balls and pushed at obscure spewage.

So this was the reverse of dazzling Nauset.
The flip of a coin – the flip of an ocean fallen
Dream-face down. And here, at my feet, in the suds,
The other face, the real, staring upwards.

The Picture of Little T. C. in a Prospect of Flowers

I

See with what simplicity
This nymph begins her golden days!
In the green grass she loves to lie,
And there with her fair aspect tames
The wilder flowers, and gives them names:
But only with the roses plays;
      And them does tell
What colour best becomes them, and what smell.

2

Who can foretell for what high cause
This Darling of the Gods was born!
Yet this is she whose chaster laws
The wanton Love shall one day fear,
And, under her command severe,
See his bow broke and ensigns torn.
      Happy, who can
Appease this virtuous enemy of man!

3

O, then let me in time compound,
And parley with those conquering eyes;
Ere they have tried their force to wound,
Ere, with their glancing wheels, they drive
In triumph over hearts that strive,
And them that yield but more despise.
      Let me be laid,
Where I may see thy glories from some shade.

4

Meantime, whilst every verdant thing
Itself does at thy beauty charm,
Reform the errors of the spring;
Make that the tulips may have share
Of sweetness, seeing they are fair;
And roses of their thorns disarm:
>> But most procure
That violets may a longer age endure.

5

But, O young beauty of the woods,
Whom Nature courts with fruits and flowers,
Gather the flowers, but spare the buds;
Lest Flora angry at thy crime,
To kill her infants in their prime,
Do quickly make the example yours;
>> And, ere we see,
Nip in the blossom all our hopes and thee.

From a Childhood

The darkness was a richness in the room
where the boy sat, hidden, by himself.
And when the mother entered, as in a dream,
a thin glass trembled on the silent shelf.
She felt as if the room betrayed her, but
she kissed her boy and murmured: Are you here?
Then both glanced shyly at the dark clavier,
for often in the evening she would sing
a song in which the child was strangely caught.

He sat so quietly, his gaze bent low
upon her hands, weighed down with heavy rings,
moving along the white keys as men go
heavily through deep drifts of snow.

translated by C. F. MacIntyre

CÉSAR VALLEJO

To My Brother Miguel
in memoriam

Brother, today I sit on the brick bench outside the house,
where you make a bottomless emptiness.
I remember we used to play at this hour of the day, and mama
would calm us: 'There now, boys . . .'

Now I go hide
as before, from all these evening
prayers, and I hope that you will not find me.
In the parlor, the entrance hall, the corridors.
Later, you hide, and I do not find you.
I remember we made each other cry,
brother, in that game.

Miguel, you hid yourself
one night in August, nearly at daybreak,
but instead of laughing when you hid, you were sad.
And your other heart of those dead afternoons
is tired of looking and not finding you. And now
shadows fall on the soul.

Listen, brother, don't be too late
coming out. All right? Mama might worry.

Translated by John Knoepfle and James Wright

The Little Brother

God! how they plague his life, the three damned sisters,
Throwing stones at him out of the cherry trees,
Pulling his hair, smudging his exercises,
Whispering. How passionately he sees
His spilt minnows flounder in the grass.

There will be sisters subtler far than these,
Baleful and dark, with slender, cared-for hands,
Who will not smirk and babble in the trees,
But feed him with sweet words and provocations,
And in his sleep practise their sorceries,
Appearing in the form of ragged clouds
And at the corners of malignant seas.

As with his wounded life he goes alone
To the world's end, where even tears freeze,
He will in bitter memory and remorse
Hear the lost sisters innocently tease.

JOHN CROWE RANSOM

Bells for John Whiteside's Daughter

There was such speed in her little body,
And such lightness in her footfall,
It is no wonder her brown study
Astonishes us all.

Her wars were bruited in our high window.
We looked among orchard trees and beyond
Where she took arms against her shadow,
Or harried unto the pond

The lazy geese, like a snow cloud
Dripping their snow on the green grass,
Tricking and stopping, sleepy and proud,
Who cried in goose, Alas,

For the tireless heart within the little
Lady with rod that made them rise
From their noon apple-dreams and scuttle
Goose-fashion under the skies!

But now go the bells, and we are ready,
In one house we are sternly stopped
To say we are vexed at her brown study,
Lying so primly propped.

The Boy Actor

I can remember. I can remember.
The months of November and December
   Were filled for me with peculiar joys
So different from those of other boys
   For other boys would be counting the days
Until end of term and holiday times
   But I was acting in Christmas plays
While they were taken to pantomimes.
   I didn't envy their Eton suits,
Their children's dances and Christmas trees.
   My life had wonderful substitutes
For such conventional treats as these.
   I didn't envy their country larks,
Their organized games in panelled halls:
   While they made snow-men in stately parks
I was counting the curtain calls.

     I remember the auditions, the nerve-racking auditions:
     Darkened auditorium and empty, dusty stage,
     Little girls in ballet dresses practising 'positions',
     Gentlemen with pince-nez asking you your age.
     Hopefulness and nervousness struggling within you,
     Dreading that familiar phrase, 'Thank you dear, no
        more.'
     Straining every muscle, every tendon, every sinew
     To do your dance much better than you'd ever done
        before.
     Think of your performance. Never mind the others,
     Never mind the pianist, talent must prevail.

Never mind the baleful eyes of other children's mothers
Glaring from the corners and willing you to fail.

I can remember. I can remember.
The months of November and December
　　Were more significant to me
Than other months could ever be
　　For they were the months of high romance
When destiny waited on tip-toe,
　　When every boy actor stood a chance
Of getting into a Christmas show,
　　Not for me the dubious heaven
Of being some prefect's protégé!
　　Not for me the Second Eleven.
For me, two performances a day.

　　Ah those first rehearsals! Only very few lines:
　　Rushing home to mother, learning them by heart,
　　'Enter Left through window' – Dots to mark the cue lines:
　　'Exit with the others' – Still it *was* a part.
　　Opening performance; legs a bit unsteady,
　　Dedicated tension, shivers down my spine,
　　Powder, grease and eye-black, sticks of make-up ready
　　Leichner number three and number five and number
　　　　nine.
　　World of strange enchantment, magic for a small boy
　　Dreaming of the future, reaching for the crown,
　　Rigid in the dressing-room, listening for the call-boy
　　'Overture Beginners – Everybody Down!'

I can remember. I can remember.
The months of November and December,
　　Although climatically cold and damp,
Meant more to me than Aladdin's lamp.

I see myself, having got a job,
Walking on wings along the Strand,
Uncertain whether to laugh or sob
And clutching tightly my mother's hand,
    I never cared who scored the goal
Or which side won the silver cup,
    I never learned to bat or bowl
But I heard the curtain going up.

Elvis Presley

Two minutes long it pitches through some bar:
Unreeling from a corner box, the sigh
Of this one, in his gangling finery
And crawling sideburns, wielding a guitar.

The limitations where he found success
Are ground on which he, panting, stretches out
In turn, promiscuously, by every note.
Our idiosyncrasy and likeness.

We keep ourselves in touch with a mere dime:
Distorting hackneyed words in hackneyed songs
He turns revolt into a style, prolongs
The impulse to a habit of the time.

Whether he poses or is real, no cat
Bothers to say: the pose held is a stance,
Which, generation of the very chance
It wars on, may be posture for combat.

My Cat, Jeoffrey

For I will consider my Cat Jeoffrey.

For he is the servant of the Living God, duly and daily
serving him.

For at the First glance of the glory of God in the East he
worships in his way.

For is this done by wreathing his body seven times round
with elegant quickness.

For then he leaps up to catch the musk, which is the blessing
of God upon his prayer.

For he rolls upon prank to work it in.

For having done duty and received blessing he begins to
consider himself.

For this he performs in ten degrees.

For first he looks upon his fore-paws to see if they are clean.

For secondly he kicks up behind to clear away there.

For thirdly he works it upon stretch with the fore-paws
extended.

For fourthly he sharpens his paws by wood.

For fifthly he washes himself.

For sixthly he rolls upon wash.

For Seventhly he fleas himself, that he may not be
interrupted upon the beat.

For Eighthly he rubs himself against a post.

For Ninthly he looks up for his instructions.

For Tenthly he goes in quest of food.

For having consider'd God and himself he will consider his
neighbour.

For if he meets another cat he will kiss her in kindness.

For when he takes his prey he plays with it to give it a
    chance.
For one mouse in seven escapes by his dallying.
For when his day's work is done his business more properly
    begins.
For he keeps the Lord's watch in the night against the
    adversary.
How he counteracts the powers of darkness by his electrical
    skin and glaring eyes.
For he counteracts the Devil, who is death, by brisking
    about the life.
For in the morning orisons he loves the sun and the sun
    loves him.
For he is the tribe of Tiger.
For the Cherub Cat is a term of the Angel Tiger.
For he has the subtlety and hissing of a serpent, which in
    goodness he suppresses.
For he will not do destruction, if he is well fed, neither will
    he spit without provocation.
For he purrs in thankfulness, when God tells him he's a good
    Cat.
For he is an instrument for the children to learn
    benevolence upon.
For every house is incomplete without him and a blessing is
    lacking in the spirit.
For the Lord commanded Moses concerning the cats at the
    departure of the Children of Israel from Egypt.
For every family had one cat at least in the bag.
For the English Cats are the best in Europe.
For he is the cleanest in the use of his fore-paws of any
    quadrupede.
For the dexterity of his defence is an instance of the love of
    God to him exceedingly.

For he is the quickest to his mark of any creature.

For he is tenacious of his point.

For he is a mixture of gravity and waggery.

For he knows that God is his Saviour.

For there is nothing sweeter than his peace when at rest.

For there is nothing brisker than his life in motion.

For he is of the Lord's poor and so indeed is he called by
benevolence perpetually – Poor Jeoffrey! poor Jeoffrey!
the rat has bit thy throat.

For I bless the name of the Lord Jesus that Jeoffrey is better.

For the divine spirit comes about his body to sustain it in
complete cat.

For his tongue is exceedingly pure so that it has in purity
what it wants in music.

For he is docile and can learn certain things.

For he can set up with gravity which is patience upon
approbation.

For he can fetch and carry, which is patience in
employment.

For he can jump over a stick which is patience upon proof
positive.

For he can spraggle upon waggle at the word of command.

For he can jump from an eminence into his master's bosom.

For he can catch the cork and toss it again.

For he is hated by the hypocrite and miser.

For the former is affraid of detection.

For the latter refuses the charge.

For he camels his back to bear the first notion of business.

For he is good to think on, if a man would express himself
neatly.

For he made a great figure in Egypt for his signal services.

For he killed the Ichneumon-rat very pernicious by land.

For his ears are so acute that they sting again.

For from this proceeds the passing quickness of his
   attention.
For by stroking of him I have found out electricity.
For I perceived God's light upon him both wax and fire.
For the Electrical fire is the spiritual substance, which God
   sends from heaven to sustain the bodies both of man and
   beast.
For God has blessed him in the variety of his movements.
For, tho he cannot fly, he is an excellent clamberer.
For his motions upon the face of the earth are more than
   any other quadrupede.
For he can tread to all the measures upon the music.
For he can swim for life.
For he can creep.

From Jubilate Agno

And now the house-dog stretched once more

And now the house-dog stretched once more
His limbs upon the glowing floor;
The children half resumed their play,
Though from the warm hearth scared away.
The goodwife left her spinning-wheel,
And spread with smiles the evening meal;
The shepherd placed a seat and pressed
To their poor fare his unknown guest.
And he unclasped his mantle now,
And raised the covering from his brow;
Said, 'Voyagers by land and sea
Were seldom feasted daintily';
And checked his host by adding stern
He'd no refinement to unlearn.
A silence settled on the room;
The cheerful welcome sank to gloom;
But not those words, though cold and high,
So froze their hospitable joy.
No – there was something in his face,
Some nameless thing they could not trace,
And something in his voice's tone
Which turned their blood as chill as stone.
The ringlets of his long black hair
Fell o'er a cheek most ghastly fair.
Youthful he seemed – but worn as they
Who spend too soon their youthful day.
When his glance drooped, 'twas hard to quell
Unbidden feelings' sudden swell;
And pity scarce her tears could hide,

So sweet that brow, with all its pride;
But when upraised his eye would dart
An icy shudder through the heart.
Compassion changed to horror then
And fear to meet that gaze again.
It was not hatred's tiger-glare,
Nor the wild anguish of despair;
It was not useless misery
Which mocks at friendship's sympathy.
No – lightning all unearthly shone
Deep in that dark eye's circling zone,
Such withering lightning as we deem
None but a spectre's look may beam;
And glad they were when he turned away
And wrapt him in his mantle grey,
Leant down his head upon his arm
And veiled from view his basilisk charm.

Winter: My Secret

I tell my secret? No indeed, not I:
Perhaps some day, who knows?
But not to-day; it froze, and blows, and snows
And you're too curious: fie!
You want to hear it? well:
Only, my secret's mine, and I won't tell.

Or, after all, perhaps there's none:
Suppose there is no secret after all,
But only just my fun.
To-day's a nipping day, a biting day;
In which one wants a shawl,
A veil, a cloak, and other wraps:
I cannot ope to every one who taps,
And let the draughts come whistling through my hall;
Come bounding and surrounding me,
Come buffeting, astounding me,
Nipping and clipping through my wraps and all.
I wear my mask for warmth: who ever shows
His nose to Russian snows
To be pecked at by every wind that blows?
You would not peck? I thank you for good will,
Believe, but leave that truth untested still.

Spring's an expansive time: yet I don't trust
March with its peck of dust,
Nor April with its rainbow-crowned brief showers,
Nor even May, whose flowers
One frost may wither through the sunless hours.
Perhaps some languid summer day,

When drowsy birds sing less and less,
And golden fruit is ripening to excess,
If there's not much sun nor too much cloud,
And the warm wind is neither still nor loud,
Perhaps my secret I may say,
Or you may guess.

The Ballad of Villon and Fat Madge

' 'Tis no sin for a man to labour in his vocation.'
'The night cometh, when no man can work.'

What though the beauty I love and serve be cheap,
    Ought you to take me for a beast or fool?
All things a man could wish are in her keep;
    For her I turn swashbuckler in love's school.
    When folk drop in, I take my pot and stool
And fall to drinking with no more ado.
I fetch them bread, fruit, cheese, and water, too;
    I say all's right so long as I'm well paid;
'Look in again when your flesh troubles you,
    Inside this brothel where we drive our trade.'

But soon the devil's among us flesh and fell,
    When penniless to bed comes Madge my whore;
I loathe the very sight of her like hell.
    I snatch gown, girdle, surcoat, all she wore,
    And tell her, these shall stand against her score.
She grips her hips with both hands, cursing God,
Swearing by Jesus' body, bones, and blood,
    That they shall not. Then I, no whit dismayed,
Cross her cracked nose with some stray shiver of wood
    Inside this brothel where we drive our trade.

When all's up she drops me a windy word,
    Bloat like a beetle puffed and poisonous:
Grins, thumps my pate, and calls me dickey-bird,
    And cuffs me with a fist that's ponderous.
    We sleep like logs, being drunken both of us;
Then when we wake her womb begins to stir;

To save her seed she gets me under her
   Wheezing and whining, flat as planks are laid:
And thus she spoils me for a whoremonger
   Inside this brothel where we drive our trade.

Blow, hail or freeze, I've bread here baked rent free!
Whoring's my trade, and my whore pleases me;
   Bad cat, bad rat; we're just the same if weighed.
We that love filth, filth follows us, you see;
Honour flies from us, as from her we flee
   Inside this brothel where we drive our trade.

     I bequeath likewise to fat Madge
       This little song to learn and study;
     By God's head she's a sweet fat fadge,
       Devout and soft of flesh and ruddy;
     I love her with my soul and body,
     So doth she me, sweet dainty thing.
       If you fall in with such a lady,
       Read it, and give it her to sing.

     translated by Algernon Charles Swinburne

Epistle to Miss Blount, on Her Leaving the Town, after the Coronation

As some fond virgin, whom her mother's care
Drags from the town to wholesome country air,
Just when she learns to roll a melting eye,
And hear a spark, yet think no danger nigh;
From the dear man unwilling she must sever,
Yet takes one kiss before she parts for ever:
Thus from the world fair *Zephalinda* flew,
Saw others happy, and with sighs withdrew;
Not that their pleasures caus'd her discontent,
She sigh'd not that They stay'd, but that She went.

She went, to plain-work, and to purling brooks,
Old-fashion'd halls, dull aunts, and croaking rooks,
She went from Op'ra, park, assembly, play,
To morning walks, and pray'rs three hours a day;
To pass her time 'twixt reading and Bohea,
To muse, and spill her solitary Tea,
Or o'er cold coffee trifle with the spoon,
Count the slow clock, and dine exact at noon;
Divert her eyes with pictures in the fire,
Hum half a tune, tell stories to the squire;
Up to her godly garret after sev'n,
There starve and pray, for that's the way to heav'n.

Some Squire, perhaps, you take a delight to rack;
Whose game is Whisk, whose treat a toast in sack,
Who visits with a gun, presents you birds,
Then gives a smacking buss, and cries – No words!
Or with his hound comes hollowing from the stable,
Makes love with nods, and knees beneath a table;

Whose laughs are hearty, tho' his jests are coarse,
And loves you best of all things – but his horse.
    In some fair evening, on your elbow laid,
You dream of triumphs in the rural shade;
In pensive thought recall the fancy'd scene,
See Coronations rise on ev'ry green;
Before you pass th' imaginary sights
Of Lords, and Earls, and Dukes, and garter'd Knights,
While the spread Fan o'ershades your closing eyes;
Then give one flirt, and all the vision flies.
Thus vanish sceptres, coronets, and balls,
And leave you in lone woods, or empty walls.
    So when your slave, at some dear, idle time,
(Not plagu'd with headaches, or the want of rhyme)
Stands in the streets, abstracted from the crew,
And while he seems to study, thinks of you:
Just when his fancy points your sprightly eyes,
Or sees the blush of soft *Parthenia* rise,
Gay pats my shoulder, and you vanish quite;
Streets, chairs, and coxcombs rush upon my sight;
Vex'd to be still in town, I knit my brow,
Look sour, and hum a tune – as you may now.

A Beautiful Young Nymph Going to Bed

Corinna, Pride of *Drury-Lane*,
For whom no Shepherd sighs in vain;
Never did *Covent Garden* boast
So bright a batter'd, strolling Toast;
No drunken Rake to pick her up,
No Cellar where on Tick to sup;
Returning at the Midnight Hour;
Four Stories climbing to her Bow'r;
Then, seated on a three-legg'd Chair,
Takes off her artificial Hair:
Now, picking out a Crystal Eye,
She wipes it clean, and lays it by.
Her Eye-Brows from a Mouse's Hyde,
Stuck on with Art on either Side,
Pulls off with Care, and first displays 'em,
Then in a Play-Book smoothly lays 'em.
Now dextrously her Plumpers draws,
That serve to fill her hollow Jaws.
Untwists a Wire; and from her Gums
A Set of Teeth completely comes.
Pulls out the Rags contriv'd to prop
Her flabby Dugs and down they drop.
Proceeding on, the lovely Goddess
Unlaces next her Steel-Rib'd Bodice;
Which by the Operator's Skill,
Press down the Lumps, the Hollows fill,
Up goes her Hand, and off she slips
The Bolsters that supply her Hips.
With gentlest Touch, she next explores

Her Shankers, Issues, running Sores,
Effects of many a sad Disaster;
And then to each applies a Plaister,
But must, before she goes to Bed,
Rub off the Dawbs of White and Red;
And smooth the Furrows in her Front,
With greasy Paper stuck upon't.
She takes a *Bolus* e'er she sleeps;
And then between two Blankets creeps.
With Pains of Love tormented lies;
Or if she chance to close her Eyes,
Of *Bridewell* and the *Compter* dreams,
And feels the Lash, and faintly screams;
Or, by a faithless Bully drawn,
At some Hedge-Tavern lies in Pawn;
Or to *Jamaica* seems transported,
Alone, and by no Planter courted;
Or, near *Fleet-Ditch's* oozy brinks,
Surrounded with a Hundred Stinks,
Belated, seems on watch to lye,
And snap some Cully passing by;
Or, struck with Fear, her Fancy runs
On Watchmen, Constables and Duns,
From whom she meets with frequent Rubs;
But, never from Religious Clubs;
Whose Favour she is sure to find,
Because she pays them all in Kind.

    Corinna wakes. A dreadful Sight!
Behold the Ruins of the Night!
A wicked Rat her Plaister stole,
Half eat, and dragg'd it to his Hole.
The Crystal Eye, alas, was miss't;
And *Puss* had on her Plumpers pisst.

A Pigeon pick'd her Issue-Peas;
And *Shock* her Tresses fill'd with Fleas.
    The Nymph, tho' in this mangled Plight,
Must ev'ry Morn her Limbs unite.
But how shall I describe her Arts
To recollect the scatter'd Parts?
Or shew the Anguish, Toil, and Pain,
Of gath'ring up herself again?
The bashful Muse will never bear
In such a Scene to interfere.
Corinna in the Morning, dizen'd.
Who sees, will spew; who smells, be poison'd.

shankers, *sores*; front, *forehead*; compter, *prison*; bully, *pimp*;
rubs, *confrontations*; religious clubs, *reformation groups*;
issue-peas, *surgical dressings*.

Mews Flat Mona
A Memory of the 'Twenties

She flourished in the 'Twenties, 'hectic' days of Peace,
'Twas good to be alive then, and to be a Baronet's Niece.
Oh, Mona! it's not so good now!

Mona in the last war was a Problem Child,
She roared and ranted, so they let her run wild;
Expelled from St Faith's, she was shot from a gun
At a circus she'd joined, for a bet, at Lausanne.
Oh, Mona! they're rid of you now!

She had her hair bobbed, when the fashion began,
To catch the eye of some soft-hearted man.
Oh, Mona! they're just as soft now!

A man was caught; she ran off in her teens
With the heir to a fortune from adding-machines,
But he failed to reckon up the wear and tear,
By the time she left him he had iron-grey hair.
Oh, Mona! you're subtracted now!

Mona took a flat in a Mayfair Mews;
To do that then was to be in the news.
Oh, Mona! it wouldn't be now!

The walls were of glass and the floor of pewter,
This was thought 'intriguing', but the bathroom was
cuter;

On a sofa upholstered in human skin
Mona did researches in original sin.
Oh, Mona! they're concluded now!

Mews Flat Mona, as a Bright Young Thing,
Led a pet crocodile about on a string;
In a green cloche hat and a knee-length skirt
She dragged the tired reptile till it was inert.
Oh, Mona! it's gone to earth now!

Diamond bracelets blazed on her wrists
(They were not presented by misogynists)
And Mona got engaged to a scatterbrained peer,
His breach of promise cost him pretty dear.
Oh, Mona! he couldn't pay now!

When she gave a dance she engaged three bands,
And she entered the Ritz once walking on her hands,
She drove round London in a crimson Rolls,
'The soul of every party' – as if parties had souls!
Oh, Mona! the party's over now!

Mews Flat Mona, as a Period Vamp,
Spent a week-end in a nudist camp;
Her barefaced behaviour upset the crowd
And she came back sunburnt under a cloud.
Oh, Mona! you're in the shade now!

She babbled of Coué and also of Freud,
But her book of engagements was the one she enjoyed.
Oh, Mona! you've no dates now!

She lived for a time with an Irish Jew
And thought it an 'amusing' thing to do;
He taught her to take morphia, heroin, and 'snow',
A giddy life, but she was used to vertigo.
Oh, Mona! no pipe-dreams now!

Too bright were her eyes, the pace was too fast,
Both ends of the candle were burnt out at last.
   Oh, Mona! you're blacked out now!

She stepped from the top of an Oxford Street store;
She might well have waited a split second more
For she fell like a bomb on an elderly curate
And his life was over before he could insure it.
   Oh, Mona! you're exploded now!

When they came with a shovel to shift her remains
They found a big heart but no vestige of brains.
   Oh, Mona! that accounts for you now!

STEVIE SMITH

Do Take Muriel Out

Do take Muriel out
She is looking so glum
Do take Muriel out
All her friends have gone.

And after too much pressure
Looking for them in the Palace
She goes home to too much leisure
And this is what her life is.

All her friends are gone
And she is alone
And she looks for them where they have never been
And her peace is flown.

Her friends went into the forest
And across the river
And the desert took their footprints
And they went with a believer.

Ah they are gone they were so beautiful
And she can not come to them
And she kneels in her room at night
Crying, Amen.

Do take Muriel out
Although your name is Death
She will not complain
When you dance her over the blasted heath.

Sun and Fun
Song of a Night-Club Proprietress

I walked into the night-club in the morning;
   There was kummel on the handle of the door.
The ashtrays were unemptied,
The cleaning unattempted,
   And a squashed tomato sandwich on the floor.

I pulled aside the thick magenta curtains
   – So Regency, so Regency, my dear –
And a host of little spiders
Ran a race across the ciders
   To a box of baby 'pollies by the beer.

Oh sun upon the summer-going by-pass
   Where ev'rything is speeding to the sea,
And wonder beyond wonder
That here where lorries thunder
   The sun should ever percolate to me.

When Boris used to call in his Sedanca,
   When Teddy took me down to his estate
When my nose excited passion,
When my clothes were in the fashion,
   When my beaux were never cross if I was late,

There was sun enough for lazing upon beaches,
   There was fun enough for far into the night.
But I'm dying now and done for,
What on earth was all the fun for?
   For I'm old and ill and terrified and tight.

Friedrich

Friedrich, at twenty-two,
Sumptuously bankrupt,
Bought a garage:
Every fuel-tank ailing.

Also a mobilisation
Of motor-bikes. Owes
A butcher's ransom
Of Deutschmarks. Has bikes

In the bathroom, kitchen,
Closets, bedroom.
To use the landing lavatory you have
To aim between two Suzukis.

He's a graceful mover; slim as
A fern-tree. Has a dancer's
Small bottom. His wife Peachy's
A sorceress. They don't

Say much when I'm around
But I know they've something
Going between them better than
Collected Poems, a T. S. B. account,

Twelve lines in *Gems
Of Modern Quotations*
And two (not war) medals.
Today, Friedrich

Sat for three hours
Earthed by the ears

To a Sony Sound System.
I couldn't hear

The music, only
Him singing. It was like
A speared hog. *Love,*
Skirled Friedrich, *'s when a cloud*

Fades in the blue
'N there's me, 'n there's you.
'N it's true.
Peachy brings in Coke

And Black Forest *gâteau.*
Their mutual gaze
Broaches each other's eye.

Next week he'll be Vasco da Gama.

Alfred Corning Clark
(1916–1961)

You read the *New York Times*
every day at recess,
but in its dry
obituary, a list
of your wives, nothing is news,
except the ninety-five
thousand dollar engagement ring
you gave the sixth.
Poor rich boy,
you were unseasonably adult
at taking your time,
and died at forty-five.
Poor Al Clark,
behind your enlarged,
hardly recognizable photograph,
I feel the pain.
You were alive. You are dead.
You wore bow-ties and dark
blue coats, and sucked
wintergreen or cinnamon lifesavers
to sweeten your breath.
There must be something –
some one to praise
your triumphant diffidence,
your refusal of exertion,
the intelligence
that pulsed in the sensitive,
pale concavities of your forehead.

You never worked,
and were third in the form.
I owe you something –
I was befogged,
and you were too bored,
quick and cool to laugh.
You are dear to me, Alfred;
our reluctant souls united
in our unconventional
illegal games of chess
on the St Mark's quadrangle.
You usually won –
motionless
as a lizard in the sun.

E. A. ROBINSON

Fleming Helphenstine

At first I thought there was a superfine
Persuasion in his face; but the free glow
That filled it when he stopped and cried, 'Hollo!'
Shone joyously, and so I let it shine.
He said his name was Fleming Helphenstine,
But be that as it may; – I only know
He talked of this and that and So-and-So,
And laughed and chaffed like any friend of mine.

But soon, with a queer, quick frown, he looked at me,
And I looked hard at him; and there we gazed
In a strained way that made us cringe and wince:
Then, with a wordless clogged apology
That sounded half confused and half amazed,
He dodged, – and I have never seen him since.

Aspects of Robinson

Robinson at cards at the Algonquin; a thin
Blue light comes down once more outside the blinds.
Gray men in overcoats are ghosts blown past the door.
The taxis streak the avenues with yellow, orange, and red.
This is Grand Central, Mr Robinson.

Robinson on a roof above the Heights; the boats
Mourn like the lost. Water is slate, far down.
Through sounds of ice cubes dropped in glass, an osteopath,
Dressed for the links, describes an old Intourist tour.
– Here's where old Gibbons jumped from, Robinson.

Robinson walking in the Park, admiring the elephant.
Robinson buying the *Tribune*, Robinson buying *The Times*.
  Robinson
Saying, 'Hello. Yes, this is Robinson. Sunday
At five? I'd love to. Pretty well. And you?'
Robinson alone at Longchamps, staring at the wall.

Robinson afraid, drunk, sobbing Robinson
In bed with a Mrs Morse. Robinson at home;
Decisions: Toynbee or luminol? Where the sun
Shines, Robinson in flowered trunks, eyes toward
The breakers. Where the night ends, Robinson in East Side
  bars.

Robinson in Glen plaid jacket, Scotch-grain shoes,
Black four-in-hand and oxford button-down,
The jeweled and silent watch that winds itself, the brief-
Case, covert topcoat, clothes for spring, all covering
His sad and usual heart, dry as a winter leaf.

Paysage Triste

The girl who mounted in the omnibus
The rainy day, and paid a penny fare
Who answered my appreciative stare
With that averted look without surprise
Which only the experienced can wear
A girl with reddish hair and faint blue eyes

An almost denizen of Leicester Square.
We could not have had her in the box with us
She would not have known how to sit, or what to wear
Yet if I close my eyes I see her moving
With loosened hair about her chamber
With naked feet passing across the skies

She would have been most crudely ill at ease
She would not have known how to sit, or what to wear
Nor, when the lights went out and the horn began
Have leaned as you did, your elbow on my knees
To prod impetuously with your fan
The smiling stripling with the pink soaped face
Who had your opera-glasses in his care.

The Farmer's Bride

Three Summers since I chose a maid,
Too young maybe – but more's to do
At harvest-time than bide and woo.
   When us was wed she turned afraid
Of love and me and all things human;
Like the shut of a winter's day.
Her smile went out, and 'twasn't a woman –
   More like a little frightened fay.
      One night, in the Fall, she runned away.

'Out 'mong the sheep, her be,' they said,
'Should properly have been abed;
But sure enough she wasn't there
Lying awake with her wide brown stare.
So over seven-acre field and up-along across the down
   We chased her, flying like a hare
Before our lanterns. To Church-Town
   All in a shiver and a scare
We caught her, fetched her home at last
   And turned the key upon her, fast.

She does the work about the house
As well as most, but like a mouse:
   Happy enough to chat and play
   With birds and rabbits and such as they,
   So long as men-folk keep away.
'Not near, not near!' her eyes beseech
When one of us comes within reach.
   The women say that beasts in stall
   Look round like children at her call.

I've hardly heard her speak at all.
Shy as a leveret, swift as he,
Straight and slight as a young larch tree,
Sweet as the first wild violets, she,
To her wild self. But what to me?

The short days shorten and the oaks are brown,
    The blue smoke rises to the low grey sky,
One leaf in the still air falls slowly down,
    A magpie's spotted feathers lie
On the black earth spread white with rime,
The berries redden up to Christmas-time.
    What's Christmas-time without there be
    Some other in the house than we!

    She sleeps up in the attic there
    Alone, poor maid. 'Tis but a stair
Betwixt us. Oh! my God! the down,
The soft young down of her, the brown,
The brown of her – her eyes, her hair, her hair!

Margery Kempe

They fled from the boisterous sobbings of Margery Kempe
With fourteen children, husband and sins behind her
Now in her white and righteous robes
Noisily full of herself and her new vision
That plunged like a thunderbolt into her unread mind
And set her middle-aged legs
On the road to the Holy Land.
She couldn't write, so she had to make a noise.
They complained and avoided her company
(Especially in church
Where she really was outrageous
In the loud expression
Of her new-found passion).
An excessive lady
She tells us herself –
Far too fond of love
Even if the lover was her husband
And he, poor fellow,
Driven to incontinence and premature senility
(Another good reason for changing her direction).
A lovely terrible person
But a bit too much on a long dusty pilgrimage –
Better to travel with her now
When many centuries tone down the din.
A quiet Dutch scholar wrote it all down for her,
Bullied, no doubt, but his careful script never wavered,
And he kept his smiles suppressed
Till the self-revealing tale was told.

BERNARD O'DONOGHUE

A Nun Takes the Veil

That morning early I ran through briars
To catch the calves that were bound for market.
I stopped the once, to watch the sun
Rising over Doolin across the water.

The calves were tethered outside the house
While I had my breakfast: the last one at home
For forty years. I had what I wanted (they said
I could), so we'd loaf bread and Marie biscuits.

We strung the calves behind the boat,
Me keeping clear to protect my style:
Confirmation suit and my patent sandals.
But I trailed my fingers in the cool green water,

Watching the puffins driving homeward
To their nests on Aran. On the Galway mainland
I tiptoed clear of the cow-dunged slipway
And watched my brothers heaving the calves

As they lost their footing. We went in a trap,
Myself and my mother, and I said goodbye
To my father then. The last I saw of him
Was a hat and jacket and a salley stick,

Driving cattle to Ballyvaughan.
He died (they told me) in the country home,
Asking to see me. But that was later:
As we trotted on through the morning mist,

I saw a car for the first time ever,
Hardly seeing it before it vanished.

I couldn't believe it, and I stood up looking
To where I could hear its noise departing

But it was only a glimpse. That night in the convent
The sisters spoilt me, but I couldn't forget
The morning's vision, and I fell asleep
With the engine humming through the open window.

Absolon *from* The Miller's Tale

Now was ther of that chirche a parissh clerk,
The which that was ycleped Absolon.
Crul was his heer, and as the gold it shoon,
And strouted as a fanne large and brode;
Ful streight and evene lay his joly shode.
His rode was reed, his eyen greye as goos.
With Poules wyndow corven on his shoos,
In hoses rede he wente fetisly.
Yclad he was ful smal and proprely
Al in a kirtel of a lyght waget;
Ful faire and thikke been the poyntes set.
And therupon he hadde a gay surplys
As whit as is the blosme upon the rys.
A myrie child he was, so God me save.
Wel koude he laten blood, and clippe and shave,
And maken a chartre of lond or acquitaunce.
In twenty manere koude he trippe and daunce
After the scole of Oxenforde tho,
And with his legges casten to and fro,
And pleyen songes on a smal rubible;
Therto he song som tyme a loud quynyble;
And as wel koude he pleye on a giterne.
In al the toun nas brewhous ne taverne
That he ne visited with his solas,
Ther any gaylard tappestere was.
But sooth to seyn, he was somdeel squaymous
Of fartyng, and of speche daungerous.

Crul, *curled*; strouted as a fanne, *stretched out like a fan*; joly, *pretty*; shode, *parted hair*; rode, *complexion*; Poules wyndow, *window of St Paul's*; corven, *carved*; fetisly, *elegantly*; smal, *tightly, in close-fitting clothes*; kirtel, *tunic*; lyght waget, *light blue*; poyntes, *laces*; surplys, *surplice (ecclesiastical gown)*; rys, *twig*; child, *young man*; so, *as*; laten blood, *let blood (as a medical treatment)*; clippe, *cut hair*; chartre, *deed*; acquitaunce, *quitance (legal release of property)*; twenty manere, *twenty ways*; After the scole, *in the style, fashion*; tho, *then*; casten, *move quickly*; rubible, *rebeck, a kind of fiddle*; quynyble, *high treble*; giterne, *cithern, a stringed instrument*; solas, *entertainment*; gaylard tappestere, *merry barmaid*; somdeel squaymous, *somewhat squeamish*; daungerous, *fastidious*.

The Description of Sir Geoffrey Chaucer

His stature was not very tall,
Lean he was, his legs were small,
Hosed within a stock of red,
A buttoned bonnet on his head,
From under which did hang, I ween,
Silver hairs both bright and sheen.
His beard was white, trimmed round,
His countenance blithe and merry found.
A sleeveless jacket large and wide,
With many plights and skirts side,
Of water camlet did he wear;
A whittle by his belt he bare,
His shoes were corned, broad before,
His inkhorn at his side he wore,
And in his hand he bore a book.
Thus did this ancient poet look.

small, *slender*; stock, *stocking*; side, *long*; water camlet, *material made of goat-hair with a wavy surface*; whittle, *knife, dagger*; corned, *pointed*.

from Livings

I

I deal with farmers, things like dips and feed.
Every third month I book myself in at
The — Hotel in —ton for three days.
The boots carries my lean old leather case
Up to a single, where I hang my hat.
One beer, and then 'the dinner', at which I read
The —*shire Times* from soup to stewed pears.
Births, deaths. For sale. Police court. Motor spares.

Afterwards, whisky in the Smoke Room: Clough,
Margetts, the Captain, Dr Watterson;
Who makes ends meet, who's taking the knock,
Government tariffs, wages, price of stock.
Smoke hangs under the light. The pictures on
The walls are comic – hunting, the trenches, stuff
Nobody minds or notices. A sound
Of dominoes from the Bar. I stand a round.

Later, the square is empty: a big sky
Drains down the estuary like the bed
Of a gold river, and the Customs House
Still has its office lit. I drowse
Between ex-Army sheets, wondering why
I think it's worth while coming. Father's dead:
He used to, but the business now is mine.
It's time for change, in nineteen twenty-nine.

from This is Your Subject Speaking

One particular night
you were prowling in front of my fireplace
half an eye on your drink, half on supper,

and in the mantelpiece litter of postcards,
ornaments, bowls of odourless pot-pourri,
discovered a jokey book-mark: 'Some say

Life's the thing, but I prefer reading.'
Jesus Christ what balls. You slewed
round on your heel to the table

almost before your anger took hold.
Later, carefully pushing your glass
through the elaborate debris of napkins

and plates shoved any old how
(so it seemed you were making a move
in chess, or planning a battle):

*You see, there's nothing to write
which is better than life itself, no matter
how life might let you down, or pass you by,*

and smiled – a sad, incredulous smile
which disallowed everything you or anyone
listening then might have wanted to add.

*

*. . . but then again,
I'm really not surprised to be alone.*

'My wife and I have asked a crowd of craps'
and 'Keep them all off'

put paid to invitations, I can tell you.
Though there was the time
(you made a fierce deleting bleep)
wrote: 'Philip; I've to be in Hull

from February second for a day or so;
I'll get to you at half past six'.
What could I do? I had a spare room
but no furniture. So out I went.

and spent a fortune on a bed,
a bed-side table, chest-of-drawers,
a looking-glass, 'that' (you grinned)
'that vase.' Anyway, he came and went,

and then a second letter: 'My dear Philip;
wonderful to see you looking well. Thank you
for your hospitality, and jazz, and drink,
and talk.' But not a word about the furniture.

Why Brownlee Left

Why Brownlee left, and where he went,
Is a mystery even now.
For if a man should have been content
It was him; two acres of barley,
One of potatoes, four bullocks,
A milker, a slated farmhouse.
He was last seen going out to plough
On a March morning, bright and early.

By noon Brownlee was famous;
They had found all abandoned, with
The last rig unbroken, his pair of black
Horses, like man and wife,
Shifting their weight from foot to
Foot, and gazing into the future.

Butch Weldy

After I got religion and steadied down
They gave me a job in the canning works,
And every morning I had to fill
The tank in the yard with gasoline,
That fed the blow-fires in the sheds
To heat the soldering irons.
And I mounted a rickety ladder to do it,
Carrying buckets full of the stuff.
One morning, as I stood there pouring,
The air grew still and seemed to heave,
And I shot up as the tank exploded,
And down I came with both legs broken,
And my eyes burned crisp as a couple of eggs.
For someone left a blow-fire going,
And something sucked the flame in the tank.
The Circuit Judge said whoever did it
Was a fellow-servant of mine, and so
Old Rhodes' son didn't have to pay me.
And I sat on the witness stand as blind
As Jack the Fiddler, saying over and over,
'I didn't know him at all.'

House Guest

The sad seamstress
who stays with us this month
is small and thin and bitter.
No one can cheer her up.
Give her a dress, a drink,
roast chicken, or fried fish –
it's all the same to her.

She sits and watches TV.
No, she watches zigzags.
'Can you adjust the TV?'
'No,' she says. No hope.
She watches on and on,
without hope, without air.

Her own clothes give us pause,
but she's not a poor orphan.
She has a father, a mother,
and all that, and she's earning
quite well, and we're stuffing
her with fattening foods.

We invite her to use the binoculars.
We say, 'Come see the jets!'
We say, 'Come see the baby!'
Or the knife grinder who cleverly
plays the National Anthem
on his wheels so shrilly.
Nothing helps.

She speaks: 'I need a little
money to buy buttons.'
She seems to think it's useless
to ask. Heavens, buy buttons,
if they'll do any good,
the biggest in the world –
by the dozen, by the gross!
Buy yourself an ice cream,
a comic book, a car!

Her face is closed as a nut,
closed as a careful snail
or a thousand-year-old seed.
Does she dream of marriage?
Of getting rich? Her sewing
is decidedly mediocre.

Please! Take our money! Smile!
What on earth have we done?
What has everyone done
and when did it all begin?
Then one day she confides
that she wanted to be a nun
and her family opposed her.

Perhaps we should let her go,
or deliver her straight off
to the nearest convent – and wasn't
her month up last week, anyway?
Can it be that we nourish
one of the Fates in our bosoms?
Clotho, sewing our lives
with a bony little foot

on a borrowed sewing machine,
and our fates will be like hers,
and our hems crooked forever?

Cinquevalli

Cinquevalli is falling, falling.
The shining trapeze kicks and flirts free,
solo performer at last.
The sawdust puffs up with a thump,
settles on a tangle of broken limbs.
St Petersburg screams and leans.
His pulse flickers with the gas-jets. He lives.

Cinquevalli has a therapy.
In his hospital bed, in his hospital chair
he holds a ball, lightly, lets it roll round his hand,
or grips it right, gauging its weight and resistance,
begins to balance it, to feel its life attached to his
by will and knowledge, invisible strings
that only he can see. He throws it
from hand to hand, always different,
always the same, always
different, always the
same.
His muscles learn to think, his arms grow very strong.

Cinquevalli in sepia
looks at me from an old postcard: bundle of enigmas.
Half faun, half military man; almond eyes, curly hair,
conventional moustache; tights, and a tunic loaded
with embroideries, tassels, chains, fringes; hand on hip
with a large signet-ring winking at the camera
but a bull neck and shoulders and a cannon-ball
at his elbow as he stands by the posing pedestal;
half reluctant, half truculent,

half handsome, half absurd,
but let me see you forget him: not to be done.

Cinquevalli is a juggler.
In a thousand theatres, in every continent,
he is the best, the greatest. After eight years perfecting
he can balance one billiard ball on another billiard ball
on top of a cue on top of a third billiard ball
in a wine-glass held in his mouth. To those
who say the balls are waxed, or flattened,
he patiently explains the trick will only work
because the spheres are absolutely true.
There is no deception in him. He is true.

Cinquevalli is juggling with a bowler,
a walking-stick, a cigar, and a coin.
Who foresees? How to please.
The last time round, the bowler
flies to his head, the stick sticks in his hand,
the cigar jumps into his mouth, the coin
lands on his foot – ah, but
is kicked into his eye
and held there as the miraculous monocle
without which the portrait would be incomplete.

Cinquevalli is practising.
He sits in his dressing-room talking to some friends,
at the same time writing a letter with one hand
and with the other juggling four balls.
His friends think of demons, but
'You could do all this,' he says,
sealing the letter with a billiard ball.

Cinquevalli is on the high wire in Odessa.
The roof cracks, he is falling, falling

into the audience, a woman breaks his fall,
he cracks her like a flea, but lives.

Cinquevalli broods in his armchair in Brixton Road.
He reads in the paper about the shells whining
at Passchendaele, imagines the mud and the dead.
He goes to the window and wonders through that dark
    evening
what is happening in Poland where he was born.
His neighbours call him a German spy.
'Kestner, Paul Kestner, that's his name!'
'Keep Kestner out of the British music-hall!'
He frowns; it is cold; his fingers seem stiff and old.

Cinquevalli tosses up a plate of soup
and twirls it on his forefinger; not a drop spills.
He laughs, and well may he laugh
who can do that. The astonished table
breathe again, laugh too, think the world
a spinning thing that spills, for a moment, no drop.

Cinquevalli's coffin sways through Brixton
only a few months before the Armistice.
Like some trick they cannot get off the ground
it seems to burden the shuffling bearers, all their arms
cross-juggle that displaced person, that man
of balance, of strength, of delights and marvels,
in his unsteady box at last into the earth.

Of Ane Blak-Moir

Lang hef I maed of ladyes quhytt;
Nou of ane blak I will indytt
   That landet furth of the last schippis,
Quhou fain wald I descryve perfytt
   My ladye with the mekle lippis:

Quhou schou is tute mowitt lyk ane aep,
And lyk a gangarall onto graep,
   And quhou hir schort catt nois up skippis,
And quhou schou schynes lyk ony saep,
   My ladye with the mekle lippis.

Quhen schou is claid in reche apparrall
Schou blinkis als brycht as ane tar barrell;
   Quhen schou was born the son tholit clippis,
The nycht be fain faucht in hir querrell,
   My ladye with the mekle lippis.

Quhai for hir saek with speir and scheld
Preiffis maest mychttelye in the feld
   Sall kis and withe hir go in grippis,
And fra thyne furth hir luff sall weld,
   My ladye with the mekle lippis.

And quhai in felde receaves schaem
And tynis thair his knychtlie naem
Sall cum behind and kis hir hippis
And nevir to uther confort claem:
My ladye with the mekle lippis.

maed, *composed poetry*; of, *about*; quhytt, *white*
nou, *now*; blak, *black woman*; indytt, *write*
landet furth of, *disembarked from*; schippis, *ships*
quhou, *how*; fain, *gladly*; descryve, *describe*; perfytt, *perfectly*
mekle, *big*
schou, *she*; tute mowitt, *with protruding lips*; aep, *ape*
gangarall, *toad*; graep, *touch*
'How she has protruding lips like an ape, and is like a toad to the touch'.
catt *cat-like*; nois, *nose*; up skippis, *turns up*
schynes, *glistens*; saep, *soap*
claid, *dressed*; reche, *rich*
blinkis, *gleams*; brycht, *brightly*
quhen, *when*; son, *sun*; tholit clippis, *suffered an eclipse*
nycht, *night*; be fain, *gladly*; faucht, *fought*; querrell, *cause*
quhai, *whoever*; saek, *sake*; scheld, *shield*
preiffis, *proves himself*; mychtellye, *bravely*; feld, *battlefield*
go in grippis, *wrestle*
fra thyne furth, *thenceforth*; luff, *love*; weld, *enjoy*
felde, *battlefield*; schaem, *dishonour*
tynis, *loses*; knychtlie, *knightly*; naem, *reputation*
hippis, *buttocks*
confort, *pleasure*; claem, *claim*
'And never claim any more pleasure from her than that'.

Resolution and Independence

There was a roaring in the wind all night;
The rain came heavily and fell in floods;
But now the sun is rising calm and bright;
The birds are singing in the distant woods;
Over his own sweet voice the stock-dove broods;
The jay makes answer as the magpie chatters;
And all the air is filled with pleasant noise of waters.

All things that love the sun are out of doors;
The sky rejoices in the morning's birth;
The grass is bright with rain-drops; – on the moors
The hare is running races in her mirth;
And with her feet she from the plashy earth
Raises a mist; that, glittering in the sun,
Runs with her all the way, wherever she doth run.

I was a Traveller then upon the moor;
I saw the hare that raced about with joy;
I heard the woods and distant waters roar;
Or heard them not, as happy as a boy:
The pleasant season did my heart employ:
My old remembrances went from me wholly;
And all the ways of men, so vain and melancholy.

But, as it sometimes chanceth, from the might
Of joys in mind that can no further go,
As high as we have mounted in delight
In our dejection do we sink as low;
To me that morning did it happen so;
And fears and fancies thick upon me came;
Dim sadness – and blind thoughts, I knew not, nor could name.

I heard the sky-lark warbling in the sky;
And I bethought me of the playful hare:
Even such a happy Child of earth am I;
Even as these blissful creatures do I fare;
Far from the world I walk, and from all care;
But there may come another day to me –
Solitude, pain of heart, distress, and poverty.

My whole life I have lived in pleasant thought,
As if life's business were a summer mood;
As if all needful things would come unsought
To genial faith, still rich in genial good;
But how can he expect that others should
Build for him, sow for him, and at his call
Love him, who for himself will take no heed at all?

I thought of Chatterton, the marvellous Boy,
The sleepless Soul that perished in his pride;
Of Him who walked in glory and in joy
Following his plough, along the mountain-side:
By our own spirits are we deified:
We Poets in our youth begin in gladness;
But thereof come in the end despondency and madness.

Now, whether it were by peculiar grace,
A leading from above, a something given,
Yet it befell that, in this lonely place,
When I with these untoward thoughts had striven,
Beside a pool bare to the eye of heaven
I saw a Man before me unawares:
The oldest man he seemed that ever wore grey hairs.

As a huge stone is sometimes seen to lie
Couched on the bald top of an eminence;
Wonder to all who do the same espy,

By what means it could thither come, and whence;
So that it seems a thing endued with sense:
Like a sea-beast crawled forth, that on a shelf
Of rock or sand reposeth, there to sun itself;

Such seemed this Man, not all alive nor dead,
Nor all asleep – in his extreme old age:
His body was bent double, feet and head
Coming together in life's pilgrimage;
As if some dire constraint of pain, or rage
Of sickness felt by him in times long past,
A more than human weight upon his frame had cast.

Himself he propped, limbs, body, and pale face,
Upon a long grey staff of shaven wood:
And, still as I drew near with gentle pace,
Upon the margin of that moorish flood
Motionless as a cloud the old Man stood,
That heareth not the loud winds when they call;
And moveth all together, if it move at all.

At length, himself unsettling, he the pond
Stirred with his staff, and fixedly did look
Upon the muddy water, which he conned,
As if he had been reading in a book:
And now a stranger's privilege I took;
And, drawing to his side, to him did say,
'This morning gives us promise of a glorious day'.

A gentle answer did the old Man make,
In courteous speech which forth he slowly drew:
And him with further words I thus bespake,
'What occupation do you there pursue?
This is a lonesome place for one like you.'

Ere he replied, a flash of mild surprise
Broke from the sable orbs of his yet-vivid eyes.

His words came feebly, from a feeble chest,
But each in solemn order followed each,
With something of a lofty utterance drest –
Choice word and measured phrase, above the reach
Of ordinary men; a stately speech;
Such as grave Livers do in Scotland use,
Religious men, who give to God and man their dues.

He told, that to these waters he had come
To gather leeches, being old and poor:
Employment hazardous and wearisome!
And he had many hardships to endure:
From pond to pond he roamed, from moor to moor;
Housing, with God's good help, by choice or chance;
And in this way he gained an honest maintenance.

The old Man still stood talking by my side;
But now his voice to me was like a stream
Scarce heard; nor word from word could I divide;
And the whole body of the Man did seem
Like one whom I had met with in a dream;
Or like a man from some far region sent,
To give me human strength, by apt admonishment.

My former thoughts returned: the fear that kills;
And hope that is unwilling to be fed;
Cold, pain, and labour, and all fleshly ills;
And mighty Poets in their misery dead.
– Perplexed, and longing to be comforted,
My question eagerly did I renew,
'How is it that you live, and what is it you do?'

He with a smile did then his words repeat;
And said that, gathering leeches, far and wide
He travelled; stirring thus about his feet
The waters of the pools where they abide.
'Once I could meet with them on every side;
But they have dwindled long by slow decay;
Yet still I persevere, and find them where I may.'

While he was talking thus, the lonely place,
The old Man's shape, and speech – all troubled me:
In my mind's eye I seemed to see him pace
About the weary moors continually,
Wandering about alone and silently.
While I these thoughts within myself pursued,
He, having made a pause, the same discourse renewed.

And soon with this he other matter blended,
Cheerfully uttered, with demeanour kind,
But stately in the main; and when he ended,
I could have laughed myself to scorn to find
In that decrepit Man so firm a mind.
'God,' said I, 'be my help and stay secure;
I'll think of the Leech-gatherer on the lonely moor!'

An Old Man's Winter Night

All out-of-doors looked darkly in at him
Through the thin frost, almost in separate stars,
That gathers on the pane in empty rooms.
What kept his eyes from giving back the gaze
Was the lamp tilted near them in his hand.
What kept him from remembering what it was
That brought him to that creaking room was age.
He stood with barrels round him – at a loss.
And having scared the cellar under him
In clomping here, he scared it once again
In clomping off; – and scared the outer night,
Which has its sounds, familiar, like the roar
Of trees and crack of branches, common things,
But nothing so like beating on a box.
A light he was to no one but himself
Where now he sat, concerned with he knew what,
A quiet light, and then not even that.
He consigned to the moon, such as she was,
So late-arising, to the broken moon
As better than the sun in any case
For such a charge, his snow upon the roof,
His icicles along the wall to keep;
And slept. The log that shifted with a jolt
Once in the stove, disturbed him and he shifted,
And eased his heavy breathing, but still slept.
One aged man – one man – can't keep a house,
A farm, a countryside, or if he can
It's thus he does it of a winter night.

The Fisherman

Although I can see him still,
The freckled man who goes
To a grey place on a hill
In grey Connemara clothes
At dawn to cast his flies,
It's long since I began
To call up to the eyes
This wise and simple man.
All day I'd looked in the face
What I had hoped 'twould be
To write for my own race
And the reality;
The living men that I hate,
The dead man that I loved,
The craven man in his seat,
The insolent unreproved,
And no knave brought to book
Who has won a drunken cheer,
The witty man and his joke
Aimed at the commonest ear,
The clever man who cries
the catch-cries of the clown,
The beating down of the wise
And great Art beaten down.

Maybe a twelvemonth since
Suddenly I began,
In scorn of this audience,
Imagining a man,
And his sun-freckled face,

And grey Connemara cloth,
Climbing up to a place
Where stone is dark under froth,
And the down-turn of his wrist
When the flies drop in the stream;
A man who does not exist,
A man who is but a dream;
And cried, 'Before I am old
I shall have written him one
Poem maybe as cold
And passionate as the dawn.'

Casualty

I

He would drink by himself
And raise a weathered thumb
Towards the high shelf,
Calling another rum
And blackcurrant, without
Having to raise his voice,
Or order a quick stout
By a lifting of the eyes
And a discreet dumb-show
Of pulling off the top;
At closing time would go
In waders and peaked cap
Into the showery dark,
A dole-kept breadwinner
But a natural for work.
I loved his whole manner,
Sure-footed but too sly,
His deadpan sidling tact,
His fisherman's quick eye
And turned, observant back.

Incomprehensible
To him, my other life.
Sometimes, on his high stool,
Too busy with his knife
At a tobacco plug
And not meeting my eye,
In the pause after a slug

He mentioned poetry.
We would be on our own
And, always politic
And shy of condescension,
I would manage by some trick
To switch the talk to eels
Or lore of the horse and cart
Or the Provisionals.

But my tentative art
His turned back watches too:
He was blown to bits
Out drinking in a curfew
Others obeyed, three nights
After they shot dead
The thirteen men in Derry.
PARAS THIRTEEN, the walls said,
BOGSIDE NIL. That Wednesday
Everybody held
Their breath and trembled.

II

It was a day of cold
Raw silence, windblown
Surplice and soutane:
Rained-on, flower-laden
Coffin after coffin
Seemed to float from the door
Of the packed cathedral
Like blossoms on slow water.
The common funeral
Unrolled its swaddling band,
Lapping, tightening

[83]

Till we were braced and bound
Like brothers in a ring.

But he would not be held
At home by his own crowd
Whatever threats were phoned,
Whatever black flags waved
I see him as he turned
In that bombed offending place,
Remorse fused with terror
In his still knowable face,
His cornered outfaced stare
Blinding in the flash.

He had gone miles away
For he drank like a fish
Nightly, naturally
Swimming towards the lure
Of warm lit-up places,
The blurred mesh and murmur
Drifting among glasses
In the gregarious smoke.
How culpable was he
That last night when he broke
Our tribe's complicity?
'Now you're supposed to be
An educated man,'
I hear him say. 'Puzzle me
The right answer to that one.'

III

I missed his funeral,
Those quiet walkers

And sideways talkers
Shoaling out of his lane
To the respectable
Purring of the hearse . . .
They move in equal pace
With the habitual
Slow consolation
Of a dawdling engine,
The line lifted, hand
Over fist, cold sunshine
On the water, the land
Banked under fog: that morning
When he took me in his boat,
The screw purling, turning
Indolent fathoms white,
I tasted freedom with him.
To get out early, haul
Steadily off the bottom,
Dispraise the catch, and smile
As you find a rhythm
Working you, slow mile by mile,
Into your proper haunt
Somewhere, well out, beyond . . .

Dawn-sniffing revenant,
Plodder through midnight rain,
Question me again.

R. S. THOMAS

The Gap in the Hedge

That man, Prytherch, with the torn cap,
I saw him often, framed in the gap
Between two hazels with his sharp eyes,
Bright as thorns, watching the sunrise
Filling the valley with its pale yellow
Light, where the sheep and the lambs went haloed
With grey mist lifting from the dew.
Or was it a likeness that the twigs drew
With bold pencilling upon that bare
Piece of sky? For he's still there
At early morning, when the light is right
And I look up suddenly at a bird's flight.

OLIVER GOLDSMITH

David Garrick

Here lies David Garrick, describe me, who can,
An abridgment of all that was pleasant in man;
As an actor, confess'd without rival to shine:
As a wit, if not first, in the very first line:
Yet, with talents like these, and an excellent heart,
The man had his failings, a dupe to his art.
Like an ill-judging beauty, his colours he spread,
And beplaster'd with rouge his own natural red.
On the stage he was natural, simple, affecting;
'Twas only that when he was off he was acting.
With no reason on earth to go out of his way,
He turn'd and he varied full ten times a day.
Though secure of our hearts, yet confoundedly sick
If they were not his own by finessing and trick,
He cast off his friends, as a huntsman his pack,
For he knew when he pleas'd he could whistle them back.
Of praise a mere glutton, he swallow'd what came,
And the puff of a dunce he mistook it for fame;
Till his relish grown callous, almost to disease,
Who pepper'd the highest was surest to please.
But let us be candid, and speak out our mind,
If dunces applauded, he paid them in kind.
Ye Kenricks, ye Kellys, and Woodfalls so grave,
What a commerce was yours, while you got and you gave!
How did Grub-street re-echo the shouts that you rais'd,
While he was be-Roscius'd, and you were be-prais'd!
But peace to his spirit, wherever it flies,
To act as an angel, and mix with the skies:
Those poets, who owe their best fame to his skill,

[87]

Shall still be his flatterers, go where he will.
Old Shakespeare, receive him, with praise and with love,
And Beaumonts and Bens be his Kellys above.

THOMAS HARDY

In Church

'And now to God the Father,' he ends,
And his voice thrills up to the topmost tiles:
Each listener chokes as he bows and bends,
And emotion pervades the crowded aisles.
Then the preacher glides to the vestry-door,
And shuts it, and thinks he is seen no more.

The door swings softly ajar meanwhile,
And a pupil of his in the Bible class,
Who adores him as one without gloss or guile,
Sees her idol stand with a satisfied smile
And re-enact at the vestry-glass
Each pulpit gesture in deft dumb-show
That had moved the congregation so.

You Don't Know What Love Is
(an evening with Charles Bukowski)

You don't know what love is Bukowski said
I'm 51 years old look at me
I'm in love with this young broad
I got it bad but she's hung up too
so it's all right man that's the way it should be
I get in their blood and they can't get me out
They try everything to get away from me
but they all come back in the end
They all came back to me except
the one I planted
I cried over that one
but I cried easy in those days
Don't let me get onto the hard stuff man
I get mean then
I could sit here and drink beer
with you hippies all night
I could drink ten quarts of this beer
and nothing it's like water
But let me get onto the hard stuff
and I'll start throwing people out windows
I'll throw anybody out the window
I've done it
But you don't know what love is
You don't know because you've never
been in love it's that simple
I got this young broad see she's beautiful
She calls me Bukowski
Bukowski she says in this little voice

and I say What
But you don't know what love is
I'm telling you what it is
but you aren't listening
There isn't one of you in this room
would recognize love if it stepped up
and buggered you in the ass
I used to think poetry readings were a copout
Look I'm 51 years old and I've been around
I *know* they're a copout
but I said to myself Bukowski
starving is even more of a copout
So there you are and nothing is like it should be
That fellow what's his name Galway Kinnell
I saw his picture in a magazine
He has a handsome mug on him
but he's a *teacher*
Christ can you imagine
But then you're teachers too
here I am insulting you already
No I haven't heard of him
or him either
They're all termites
Maybe it's ego I don't read much anymore
but these people who build
reputations on five or six books
termites
Bukowski she says
Why do you listen to classical music all day
Can't you hear her saying that
Bukowski why do you listen to classical music all day
That surprises you doesn't it
You wouldn't think a crude bastard like me

could listen to classical music all day
Brahms Rachmaninoff Bartok Telemann
Shit I couldn't write up here
Too quiet up here too many trees
I like the city that's the place for me
I put on my classical music each morning
and sit down in front of my typewriter
I light a cigar and I smoke it like this see
and I say Bukowski you're a lucky man
Bukowski you've gone through it all
and you're a lucky man
and the blue smoke drifts across the table
and I look out the window onto Delongpre Avenue
and I see people walking up and down the sidewalk
and I puff on the cigar like this
and then I lay the cigar in the ashtray like this
and take a deep breath
and I begin to write
Bukowski this is the life I say
it's good to be poor it's good to have hemorrhoids
it's good to be in love
But you don't know what it's like
You don't know what it's like to be in love
If you could see her you'd know what I mean
She thought I'd come up here and get laid
She just knew it
She told me she knew it
Shit I'm 51 years old and she's 25
and we're in love and she's jealous
Jesus it's beautiful
she said she'd claw my eyes out if I came up here and got laid
Now that's love for you
What do any of you know about it

Let me tell you something
I've met men in jail who had more style
than the people who hang around colleges
and go to poetry readings
They're bloodsuckers who come to see
if the poet's socks are dirty
or if he smells under the arms
Believe me I won't disappoint em
But I want you to remember this
there's only one poet in this room tonight
only one poet in this town tonight
maybe only one real poet in this country tonight
and that's me
What do any of you know about life
What do any of you know about anything
Which of you here has been fired from a job
or else has beaten up your broad
or else has been beaten up by your broad
I was fired from Sears and Roebuck five times
They'd fire me then hire me back again
I was a stockboy for them when I was 35
and then got canned for stealing cookies
I know what's it like I've been there
I'm 51 years old and I'm in love
This little broad she says
Bukowski
and I say What and she says
I think you're full of shit
and I say baby you understand me
She's the only broad in the world
man or woman
I'd take that from
But you don't know what love is

They all came back to me in the end too
every one of em came back
except that one I told you about
the one I planted
We were together seven years
We used to drink a lot
I see a couple of typers in this room but
I don't see any poets
I'm not surprised
You have to have been in love to write poetry
and you don't know what it is to be in love
that's your trouble
Give me some of that stuff
That's right no ice good
That's good that's just fine
So let's get this show on the road
I know what I said but I'll have just one
That tastes good
Okay then let's go let's get this over with
only afterwards don't anyone stand close
to an open window

birthday party

drinking with Norman Mailer
in his suite at the Chateau
Marmont
he tells me about a night
he had with Charlie
Chaplin.

Norman knows how to tell a
good story

then it's time to go to a
birthday party
for a producer
we are both working
for.

I tell Norman that Hollywood
terrifies me and that
I am afraid for my
god damned
soul.

we take the elevator down to
valet parking.

the valet drives up with my
car.

'I drive a BMW too,' says
Norman.

'what color?' I
ask.

'black,' he
says.

(mine is black also).

'tough guys drive black
BMWs,' I tell
him.

we get in
and I tool the
machine down
Sunset
Boulevard.

FAY HART

I Love Drunks

I love drunks, I always have.
I love guys that laugh,
hairdressers that gossip,
bouncers that scowl and tv presenters
that wear stupid wigs.
And I just love has-been rock stars that
blubber into their bourbon
about some distant drum solo
that I vaguely remember from
Ricky Munch's bedroom on acid.

I like new young designers
and entrepreneurs
who always wear the right stuff
and have cute chicks with them.
I like big homos who call me
dahling and step back,
shaking their head in admiration.
Miss Thing, one of them once said,
we have just got to get you
your own talk show.

I like somebody's dad
who spends half the night
trying to pick up girls
his daughter's age
and the other half crying into his beer
about how his little girl never
calls him anymore.
I love caterwauling women

who take their tops off
just before last call
and shake about the place
like goddesses with bourbon breath.
I love drunks, I always have.

The Talented Man
A Letter from a Lady in London to a Lady at Lausanne

Dear Alice! you'll laugh when you know it, –
    Last week, at the Duchess's ball,
I danced with the clever new poet, –
    You've heard of him, – Tully St Paul.
Miss Jonquil was perfectly frantic;
    I wish you had seen Lady Anne!
It really was very romantic,
    He *is* such a talented man!

He came up from Brazen Nose College,
    Just caught, as they call it, this spring;
And his head, love, is stuffed full of knowledge
    Of every conceivable thing.
Of science and logic he chatters,
    As fine and as fast as he can;
Though *I* am no judge of such matters,
    I'm sure he's a talented man.

His stories and jests are delightful; –
    Not stories or jests, dear, for you;
The jests are exceedingly spiteful,
    The stories not always *quite* true.
Perhaps to be kind and veracious
    May do pretty well at Lausanne;
But it never would answer, – good gracious!
    Chez nous – in a talented man.

He sneers, – how my Alice would scold him! –
    At the bliss of a sigh or a tear;
He laughed – only think! – when I told him

[99]

How we cried o'er Trevelyan last year;
I vow I was quite in a passion;
   I broke all the sticks of my fan;
But sentiment's quite out of fashion,
   It seems, in a talented man.

Lady Bab, who is terribly moral,
   Has told me that Tully is vain,
And apt – which is silly – to quarrel,
   And fond – which is sad – of champagne.
I listened, and doubted, dear Alice,
   For I saw, when my lady began,
It was only the Dowager's malice; –
   She *does* hate a talented man!

He's hideous, I own it. But fame, love,
   Is all that these eyes can adore;
He's lame, – but Lord Byron was lame, love,
   And dumpy, – but so is Tom Moore.
Then his voice, – *such* a voice! my sweet creature,
   It's like your Aunt Lucy's toucan:
But oh! what's a tone or a feature,
   When once one's a talented man?

My mother, you know, all the season,
   Has talked of Sir Geoffrey's estate;
And truly, to do the fool reason,
   He *has* been less horrid of late.
But to-day, when we drive in the carriage,
   I'll tell her to lay down her plan; –
If ever I venture on marriage,
   It must be a talented man!

P. S. – I have found, on reflection,
   One fault in my friend, – *entre nous;*

Without it, he'd just be perfection; –
  Poor fellow, he has not a *sou!*
And so, when he comes in September,
  To shoot with my uncle, Sir Dan,
I've promised mamma to remember
  He's *only* a talented man!

The mixer

With a pert moustache and a ready candid smile
He has played his way through twenty years of pubs,
Deckchairs, lounges, touchlines, junctions, homes,
And still as ever popular, he roams
Far and narrow, mimicking the style
Of other people's leisure, scattering stubs.

Colourless, when alone, and self-accused,
He is only happy in reflected light
And only real in the range of laughter;
Behind his eyes are shadows of a night
In Flanders but his mind long since refused
To let that time intrude on what came after.

So in this second war which is fearful too,
He cannot away with silence but has grown
Almost a cipher, like a Latin word
That many languages have made their own
Till it is worn and blunt and easy to construe
And often spoken but no longer heard.

THOM GUNN

Rastignac at 45

Here he is of course. It was his best
trick always: when we glance again toward
the shadow we see it has consist-
ed of him all along, lean and bored.

We denounced him so often! Yet he
comes up, and leans on one of the bars
in his dark suit, indicating the
empty glass as if we were waiters.

We fill it, and submit, more or less,
to his marvellous air of knowing
all the ropes debonair weariness
could care to handle, of 'everything

that I know I know from having done,
child, and I survive.' What calmly told
confidences of exploration
among the oversexed and titled,

or request for a few days' loan, are
we about to hear? Rastignac tell
us about Life, and what men of your
stamp endure. It must be terrible.

It is. To the left of his mouth is
an attractive scarlike line, not caused
by time unhelped. It is not the prize,
either, of a dueller's lucky thrust.

But this: time after time the fetid
taste to the platitudes of Romance

has drawn his mouth up to the one side
secretly, in a half-maddened wince.

We cannot help but pity him that
momentary convulsion; however,
the mere custom of living with it
has, for him, diminished the horror.

'I was in the Forum once at a loose end'

I was in the Forum once at a loose end
When I was seized and hauled off by my friend
Varus to meet his girl. 'A prostitute,'
I thought at the first glance, 'but rather cute,
In fact quite pretty.' Soon talk started flowing
On various topics. Then: 'How are things going
In the province of Bithynia these days? Is it
Prospering? Are you richer for your visit?'
I told the simple truth: that no one there
Can line his pocket or perfume his hair –
That goes for natives, governors and staff too,
Especially if you're in the retinue
Of some mean sod who doesn't give a thought
To his employees. 'But at least you brought
The local product back,' they said – 'a litter
With litter-men?' I, trying hard to glitter
In the girl's eyes, said, 'Oh, things weren't so bad,
Despite the rotten province that I had,
That I can't call my own eight sturdy-backed
Good litter-men. (I hadn't one, in fact,
There or in Rome, on whom I could rely
To hoist a broken bed-leg shoulder-high!).
At which the girl, just like a cheeky tart,
Said, 'Dear Catullus, could you bear to part
For an hour with them? I only want a ride
To the temple of Serapis.' 'Steady!' I cried.
'I meant to say . . . well, strictly, I was wrong
To call them *my* slaves. Actually, they belong
To a friend of mine who purchased them – that is,

To Gaius Cinna. Anyway, mine or his,
It's all the same to me; I have the loan;
I use them just as though they were my own.
But you're a tactless nuisance. It's absurd
To take a man up on a casual word.'

Translated by James Michie

The Great War Major

Mostly his conversation moved round cricket,
And after his third gin he'd demonstrate,
Umbrella for bat, playing straight
Down the line, the bar as a wicket.

Hooking and cutting, eyeglass screwed well in,
He spilled out words in a stream of nonsense,
Fingering effectively a pearl tie-pin.
Bonhomie he spent lavishly, took care of the pence.

He was one of those who would always
Rather have remained a 'blood' at school,
A brilliant allrounder, scintillating on Speech Days,
At his most serious when playing the fool.

Chambré'd again by war, back to his best,
One for the night clubs, impeccably dressed,
School with a little extra fun thrown in,
Fraüleins and a growing taste for gin.

It would never, he knew, be as good again
When, slightly wounded, his job to train
Others until there were none to train,
He waited for peace to break out again.

Returning, the form changed, his wife Honey
Went off with someone after her money,
And he had never understood how sense
Could desert a woman of such independence.

He tried to talk away his fear,
A fish out of water with a striped tie,

Clearing his throat when nothing else was clear,
Haunting his Club like an aimless fly.

Acquaintances admired him, something of a dandy
With a good war record, and always handy
For a fourth at bridge, a talk
About the old days, a brisk after-lunch walk.

But returning alone at night to his flat,
Wife, purpose gone, values no longer the same,
He would sit for hours on his bed in his hat,
Trying to recall something, unable to give it a name.

The Stalin Epigram

Our lives no longer feel ground under them.
At ten paces you can't hear our words.

But whenever there's a snatch of talk
it turns to the Kremlin mountaineer,

the ten thick worms his fingers,
his words like measures of weight,

the huge laughing cockroaches on his top lip,
the glitter of his boot-rims.

Ringed with a scum of chicken-necked bosses
he toys with the tributes of half-men.

One whistles, another meouws, a third snivels.
He pokes out his finger and he alone goes boom.

He forges decrees in a line like horseshoes,
One for the groin, one the forehead, temple, eye.

He rolls the executions on his tongue like berries.
He wishes he could hug them like big friends from home.

November 1933
Translated by Clarence Brown and W. S. Merwin

W. H. AUDEN

Epitaph on a Tyrant

Perfection, of a kind, was what he was after,
And the poetry he invented was easy to understand;
He knew human folly like the back of his hand,
And was greatly interested in armies and fleets;
When he laughed, respectable senators burst with laughter,
And when he cried the little children died in the streets.

JAMES FENTON

Dead Soldiers

When His Excellency Prince Norodom Chantaraingsey
Invited me to lunch on the battlefield
I was glad of my white suit for the first time that day.
They lived well, the mad Norodoms, they had style.
The brandy and the soda arrived in crates.
Bricks of ice, tied around with raffia,
Dripped from the orderlies' handlebars.

And I remember the dazzling tablecloth
As the APCs fanned out along the road,
The dishes piled high with frogs' legs,
Pregnant turtles, their eggs boiled in the carapace,
Marsh irises in fish sauce
And inflorescence of a banana salad.

On every bottle, Napoleon Bonaparte
Pleaded for the authenticity of the spirit.
They called the empties Dead Soldiers
And rejoiced to see them pile up at our feet.

Each diner was attended by one of the other ranks
Whirling a table-napkin to keep off the flies.
It was like eating between rows of morris dancers –
Only they didn't kick.

On my left sat the prince;
On my right, his drunken aide.
The frogs' thighs leapt into the sad purple face
Like fish to the sound of a Chinese flute.
I wanted to talk to the prince. I wish now
I had collared his aide, who was Saloth Sar's brother.

We treated him as the club bore. He was always
Boasting of his connections, boasting with a head-shake
Or by pronouncing of some doubtful phrase.
And well might he boast. Saloth Sar, for instance,
Was Pol Pot's real name. The APCs
Fired into the sugar palms but met no resistance.

In a diary, I refer to Pol Pot's brother as the Jockey Cap.
A few weeks later, I find him 'in good form
And very skeptical about Chantaraingsey.'
'But one eats well there,' I remark.
'So one should,' says the Jockey Cap:
'The tiger always eats well,
It eats the raw flesh of the deer,
And Chantaraignsey was born in the year of the tiger.
So, did they show you the things they do
With the young refugee girls?'

And he tells me how he will one day give me the gen.
He will tell me how the prince financed the casino
And how the casino brought Lon Nol to power.
He will tell me this.
He will tell me all these things.
All I must do is drink and listen.

In those days, I thought that when the game was up
The prince would be far, far away –
In a limestone faubourg, on the promenade at Nice,
Reduced in circumstances but well enough provided for.
In Paris, he would hardly require his private army.
The Jockey Cap might suffice for café warfare,
And matchboxes for APCs.

But we were always wrong in these predictions.
It was a family war. Whatever happened,

[112]

The principals were obliged to attend its issue.
A few were cajoled into leaving, a few were expelled,
And there were villains enough, but none of them
Slipped away with the swag.

For the prince was fighting Sihanouk, his nephew,
And the Jockey Cap was ranged against his brother
Of whom I remember nothing more
Than an obscure reputation for virtue.
I have been told that the prince is still fighting
Somewhere in the Cardamoms or the Elephant Mountains.
But I doubt that the Jockey Cap would have survived his
    good connections.
I think the lunches would have done for him –
Either the lunches or the dead soldiers.

Ali Ben Shufti

You want coins? Roman? Greek? Nice vase? Head of god,
    goddess?
Look, shufti here, very cheap. Two piastres? You joke.

I poke among fallen stones, molehills, the spoil
Left by the archaeologists and carelessly sieved.
I am not above ferreting out a small piece
From the foreman's basket when his back is turned.
One or two of my choicer things were acquired
During what the museum labels call 'the disturbances
Of 1941': you may call it loot,
But I keep no records of who my vendors were –
Goatherds, Johnnies in berets, Neapolitan conscripts
Hot foot out of trouble, dropping a keepsake or two.
I know a good thing, I keep a quiet ear open when
The college bodysnatchers arrive from Chicago,
Florence, Oxford, discussing periods
And measuring everything. I've even done business with
    them:
You will find my anonymous presence in the excavation
    reports
When you get to 'Finds Locally Purchased'. Without a
    B. A. –
And unable to read or write – I can date and price
Any of this rubbish. Here, from my droll pantaloons
That sag in the seat, amusing you no end,
I fetch out Tanagra heads, blue Roman beads,
A Greek lamp, bronze from Byzantium,
A silver stater faced with the head of Zeus.
I know three dozen words of English, enough French

To settle a purchase, and enough Italian
To convince the austere *dottore* he's made a bargain.
As for the past, it means nothing to me but this:
A time when things were made to keep me alive.
You are the ones who go on about it: I survive
By scratching it out with my fingers. I make you laugh
By being obsequious, roguish, battered, in fact
What you like to think of as a typical Arab.
Well, Amr Ibn el-As passed this way
Some thirteen hundred years ago, and we stayed.
I pick over what he didn't smash, and you
Pay for the leavings. That is enough for me.
You take them away and put them on your shelves
And for fifty piastres I give you a past to belong to.

Behaviour of Fish in an Egyptian Tea Garden

As a white stone draws down the fish
she on the seafloor of the afternoon
draws down men's glances and their cruel wish
for love. Slyly her red lip on the spoon

slips-in a morsel of ice-cream; her hands
white as a milky stone, white submarine
fronds, sink with spread fingers, lean
along the table, carmined at the ends.

A cotton magnate, an important fish
with great eyepouches and a golden mouth
through the frail reefs of furniture swims out
and idling, suspended, stays to watch.

A crustacean old man clamped to his chair
sits coldly near her and might see
her charms through fissures where the eyes should be
or else his teeth are parted in a stare.

Captain on leave, a lean dark mackerel
lies in the offing, turns himself and looks
through currents of sound. The flat-eyed flatfish sucks
on a straw, staring from its repose, laxly.

And gallants in shoals swim up and lag,
circling and passing near the white attraction;
sometimes pausing, opening a conversation:
fish pause so to nibble or tug.

Now the ice-cream is finished, is
paid for. The fish swim off on business:
and she sits alone at the table, a white stone
useless except to a collector, a rich man.

BERNARD SPENCER

Egyptian Dancer at Shubra

At first we heard the jingling of her ornaments
as she delayed beyond the trap of light,
and glimpsed her lingering pretence
her bare feet and the music were at difference:
and then the strings grew wild and drew her in.

And she came soft as paws and danced desire at play
or triumphing desire, and locked her hands
stretched high, and in the dance's sway
hung like a body to be flogged; then wrenched away,
or was a wave from breasts down to the knees.

And as the music built to climax and she leaned
naked in her dancing skirt, and was supreme,
her dance's stormy argument
had timid workday things for all environment;
men's awkward clothes and chairs her skin exclaimed
    against.

Dreaming in the Shanghai Restaurant

I would like to be that elderly Chinese gentleman.
He wears a gold watch with a gold bracelet,
But a shirt without sleeves or tie.
He has good luck moles on his face, but is not disfigured
    with fortune.
His wife resembles him, but is still a handsome woman,
She has never bound her feet or her belly.
Some of the party are his children, it seems,
And some his grandchildren;
No generation appears to intimidate another.
He is interested in people, without wanting to convert them
    or pervert them.
He eats with gusto, but not with lust;
And he drinks, but is not drunk.
He is content with his age, which has always suited him.
When he discusses a dish with the pretty waitress,
It is the dish he discusses, not the waitress.
The table-cloth is not so clean as to show indifference,
Not so dirty as to signify a lack of manners.
He proposes to pay the bill but knows he will not be allowed to.
He walks to the door like a man who doesn't fret about being
    respected, since he is;
A daughter or granddaughter opens the door for him,
And he thanks her.
It has been a satisfying evening. Tomorrow
Will be a satisfying morning. In between he will sleep
    satisfactorily.
I guess that for him it is peace in his time.
It would be agreeable to be this Chinese gentleman.

ALAN JENKINS

Caravaggio: Self-Portrait with Severed Head

I painted myself into a corner
of the *Martyrdom of St Matthew*
and it was as if I had proved the blade
on my own flesh and bone.
I half-hid in shadow
behind a pillar of a colonnade
and wished that I too might be turned to stone.

– As I almost was by Medusa's death-shriek,
or when, a few years after my *Matthew* triptych,
I grasped the smooth, muscly throat
of a boy who had lied
his way into my love and betrayed me,
and cut it. After the verdict of the coroner –
that my life and works posed 'a grave threat
to public morals' – I was hounded out of Rome
on a charge of homicide.

They might as well have cut off my painting arm.
Would they have put a price on my head
if they'd known how gladly I once drank
that same boy's blood,
and opened my own vein for him to drink?
If they had known how often
I had felt his thin cock stiffen
and jolt and slabber in my palm?

It hardly came as a surprise
when my 'friends in high places', bishops, cardinals even,
were afraid to stick their necks out as much as an inch –
I had repeatedly astonished their eyes

and tried to stir some compassion or pity
but would never have offered house-room
to either their piety
or their aesthetic sense:
in neither are they exactly given
to being moved, let alone to tears.

Is that little hustler for trade an icon?
Nothing could have saved him in the plague years –
not even those who feel themselves at one
with the helpless lookers-on
in my *Beheading of St John*.

To maystres Margaret Hussey

Mirry Margaret,
As mydsomer flowre,
Jentill as fawcoun
Or hawke of the towre;

With solace and gladnes,
Moche mirthe and no madnes,
All good and no badnes,
So joyously,
So maydenly,
So womanly
Her demenyng
In every thynge,
Far, far passynge
That I can endyght,
Or suffice to wryght
Or mirry Margarete,
As mydsomer flowre,
Jentyll as fawcoun
Or hawke of the towre,

As pacient and as styll,
And as full of good wyll,
As fayre Isaphill;
Colyaunder,
Swete pomaunder,
Good Cassaunder;
Stedfast of thought,
Wele made, wele wrought;
Far may be sought

Erst that ye can fynde
So corteise, so kynde
As mirry Margarete,
This midsomer flowre,
Jentyll as fawcoun
Or hawke of the towre.

The Vicar of Bray

In good King Charles's golden days,
    When loyalty no harm meant;
A furious High-Church man I was,
    And so I gained preferment.
Unto my flock I daily preached,
    'Kings are by God appointed,
And damned are those who dare resist,
    Or touch the Lord's Anointed.'
And this is Law, I will maintain
        Unto my dying day, Sir,
    That whatsoever King shall rein,
        I will be Vicar of Bray, Sir!

When royal James possessed the Crown,
    And Popery grew in fashion,
The Penal Law I hooted down,
    And read the Declaration:
The Church of Rome I found would fit
    Full well my constitution,
And I had been a Jesuit
    But for the Revolution.
        And this is Law, etc.

When William our Deliverer came
    To heal the Nation's grievance,
I turned the cat in pan again,
    And swore to him allegiance:
Old principles I did revoke,
    Set Conscience at a distance,
Passive Obedience is a joke,

A jest is Non-Resistance.
    And this is Law, etc.

When glorious Anne became our Queen,
    The Church of England's glory,
Another face of things was seen,
    And I became a Tory:
Occasional Conformists base
    I damned, and Moderation,
And thought the Church in danger was
    From such prevarication.
      And this is Law, etc.

When George in pudding time came o'er,
    And moderate men looked big, Sir,
My principles I changed once more,
    And so became a Whig, Sir:
And thus preferment I procured
    From our Faith's Great Defender,
And almost every day abjured
    The Pope and the Pretender.
      And this is Law, etc.

The illustrious House of Hanover,
    And Protestant Succession,
To these I lustily will swear,
    Whilst they can keep possession:
For in my Faith and Loyalty
    I never once will falter,
But George my lawful King shall be,
    Except the times should alter.
      And this is Law, etc.

By the Statue of King Charles at Charing Cross

Sombre and rich, the skies;
Great glooms, and starry plains.
Gently the night wind sighs;
Else a vast silence reigns.

The splendid silence clings
Around me: and around
The saddest of all kings
Crowned, and again discrowned.

Comely and calm, he rides
Hard by his own Whitehall:
Only the night wind glides:
No crowds, nor rebels, brawl.

Gone, too, his Court: and yet,
The stars his courtiers are:
Stars in their stations set;
And every wandering star.

Alone he rides, alone,
The fair and fatal king:
Dark night is all his own,
That strange and solemn thing.

Which are more full of fate:
The stars; or those sad eyes?
Which are more still and great:
Those brows; or the dark skies?

Although his whole heart yearn
In passionate tragedy:

Never was face so stern
With sweet austerity.

Vanquished in life, his death
By beauty made amends:
The passing of his breath
Won his defeated ends.

Brief life, and hapless? Nay:
Through death, life grew sublime.
Speak after sentence? Yea:
And to the end of time.

Armoured he rides, his head
Bare to the stars of doom:
He triumphs now, the dead,
Beholding London's gloom.

Our wearier spirit faints,
Vexed in the world's employ:
His soul was of the saints;
And art to him was joy.

King, tried in fires of woe!
Men hunger for thy grace:
And through the night I go,
Loving thy mournful face.

Yet, when the city sleeps;
When all the cries are still:
The stars and heavenly deeps
Work out a perfect will.

A Satyr on Charles II

I' th' isle of Britain, long since famous grown
For breeding the best cunts in Christendom,
There reigns, and oh! long may he reign and thrive,
The easiest King and best-bred man alive.
Him no ambition moves to get renown
Like the French fool, that wanders up and down
Starving his people, hazarding his crown.
Peace is his aim, his gentleness is such,
And love he loves, for he loves fucking much.

    Nor are his high desires above his strength:
His scepter and his prick are of a length;
And she may sway the one who plays with th' other,
And make him little wiser than his brother.
Poor prince! thy prick, like thy buffoons at Court,
Will govern thee because it makes thee sport.
'Tis sure the sauciest prick that e'er did swive,
The proudest, peremptoriest prick alive.
Though safety, law, religion, life lay on 't,
'Twould break through all to make its way to cunt.
Restless he rolls about from whore to whore,
A merry monarch, scandalous and poor.

    To Carwell, the most dear of all his dears,
The best relief of his declining years,
Oft he bewails his fortune, and her fate:
To love so well, and be beloved so late.
For though in her he settles well his tarse,
Yet his dull, graceless ballocks hang an arse.
This you'd believe, had I but time to tell ye
The pains it costs to poor, laborious Nelly,

Whilst she employs hands, fingers, mouth, and thighs,
Ere she can raise the member she enjoys.
　　All monarchs I hate, and the thrones they sit on,
　　From the hector of France to the cully of Britain.

Character of George Villiers, Duke of Buckingham

A man so various, that he seemed to be
Not one, but all mankind's epitome.
Stiff in opinions, always in the wrong;
Was everything by starts, and nothing long:
But, in the course of one revolving moon,
Was chemist, fiddler, statesman, and buffoon;
Then all for women, painting, rhyming, drinking,
Besides ten thousand freaks that died in thinking.
Blest madman, who could every hour employ,
With something new to wish, or to enjoy!
Railing and praising were his usual themes;
And both (to show his judgement) in extremes:
So over violent, or over civil,
That every man, with him, was God or Devil.
In squandering wealth was his peculiar art:
Nothing went unrewarded, but desert.
Beggared by fools, whom still he found too late:
He had his jest, and they had his estate.

from Absolom and Achitophel

ALEXANDER POPE

The Duke of Buckingham

In the worst inn's worst room, with mat half-hung,
The floors of plaster, and the walls of dung,
On once a flock-bed, but repaired with straw,
With tape-tied curtains, never meant to draw,
The George and Garter dangling from that bed
Where tawdry yellow strove with dirty red,
Great Villiers lies – alas, how changed from him,
That life of pleasure, and that soul of whim!
Gallant and gay, in Cliveden's proud alcove,
The bower of wanton Shrewsbury and love;
Or just as gay, at Council, in a ring
Of mimicked statesmen, and their merry King.
No Wit to flatter, left of all his store!
No fool to laugh at, which he valued more.
There, victor of his health, or fortune, friends,
And fame, this lord of useless thousands ends.

How pleasant to know Mr Lear

'How pleasant to know Mr Lear!'
  Who has written such volumes of stuff!
Some think him ill-tempered and queer,
  But a few think him pleasant enough.

His mind is concrete and fastidious,
  His nose is remarkably big;
His visage is more or less hideous,
  His beard it resembles a wig.

He has ears, and two eyes, and ten fingers,
  Leastways if you reckon two thumbs;
Long ago he was one of the singers,
  But now he is one of the dumbs.

He sits in a beautiful parlour,
  With hundreds of books on the wall
He drinks a great deal of Marsala,
  But never gets tipsy at all.

He has many friends, laymen and clerical,
  Old Foss is the name of his cat:
His body is perfectly spherical,
  He weareth a runcible hat.

When he walks in a waterproof white,
  The children run after him so!
Calling out, 'He's come out in his night-
  gown, that crazy old Englishman, oh!'

He weeps by the side of the ocean,
  He weeps on the top of the hill;

He purchases pancakes and lotion,
    And chocolate shrimps from the mill.

He reads but he cannot speak Spanish,
    He cannot abide ginger-beer:
Ere the days of his pilgrimage vanish,
    How pleasant to know Mr Lear!

Edward Lear

Left by his friend to breakfast alone on the white
Italian shore, his Terrible Demon arose
Over his shoulder; he wept to himself in the night,
A dirty landscape-painter who hated his nose.

The legions of cruel inquisitive They
Were so many and big like dogs: he was upset
By Germans and boats; affection was miles away:
But guided by tears he successfully reached his Regret.

How prodigious the welcome was. Flowers took his hat
And bore him off to introduce him to the tongs;
The demon's false nose made the table laugh; a cat
Soon had him waltzing madly, let him squeeze her hand;
Words pushed him to the piano to sing comic songs;

And children swarmed to him like settlers. He became a land.

T. S. ELIOT

Aunt Helen

Miss Helen Slingsby was my maiden aunt,
And lived in a small house near a fashionable square
Cared for by servants to the number of four.
Now when she died there was silence in heaven
And silence at her end of the street.
The shutters were drawn and the undertaker wiped his feet –
He was aware that this sort of thing had occurred before.
The dogs were handsomely provided for,
But shortly afterwards the parrot died too.
The Dresden clock continued ticking on the mantelpiece,
And the footman sat upon the dining-table
Holding the second housemaid on his knees –
Who had always been so careful while her mistress lived.

Elegy

Her face like a rain-beaten stone on the day she rolled off
With the dark hearse, and enough flowers for an alderman, –
And so she was, in her way, Aunt Tilly.

Sighs, sighs, who says they have sequence?
Between the spirit and the flesh, – what war?
She never knew;
For she asked no quarter and gave none,
Who sat with the dead when the relatives left,
Who fed and tended the infirm, the mad, the epileptic,
And, with a harsh rasp of a laugh at herself,
Faced up to the worst.

I recall how she harried the children away all the late summer
From the one beautiful thing in her yard, the peachtree;
How she kept the wizened, the fallen, the misshapen for
    herself,
And picked and pickled the best, to be left on rickety doorsteps.

And yet she died in agony,
Her tongue, at the last, thick, black as an ox's.

Terror of cops, bill collectors, betrayers of the poor, –
I see you in some celestial supermarket,
Moving serenely among the leeks and cabbages,
Probing the squash,
Bearing down, with two steady eyes,
On the quaking butcher.

The Late Richard Dadd, 1817–1886

The *Kentish Independent* of 1843
carried his pictures of his father, himself
and the scene of his crime. The first photo-journalist:
fairy-painter, father-slayer, poor, bad, mad Richard Dadd.

His extended Grand Tour took in the Holy Land
and ended in Bethlem Hospital, with its long panoptical
galleries, spider-plants, whippets and double-gaslights.
He had outlived himself at twenty-six . . .

There was one day he seemed to catch sunstroke.
He fancied the black, scorched beard of a sheik
would furnish him with some 'capital paintbrushes'.
Sailing up the Nile, on the *Hecate*,

they spent Christmas Day eating boiled eggs
and plum pudding, and playing cards for the captain's soul.
The temples at Luxor stood under a full moon, lightly boiled.
Sir Thomas got off to try and bag a crocodile.

The route up from Marseille went as the crow flies –
precipitately, a dash from ear to ear.
A fellow-traveller let him play with his collar and tie,
until he pulled out 'an excellent English razor'.

There was his watercolour, 'Dead Camel',
and a series of drawings of his friends,
all with their throats cut,
Frith, Egg, Dadd, Phillip and O'Neill.

He saw himself as a catspaw, Osiris's right-hand man
on earth. His digs in Newman Street
contained three hundred eggs, and the earth
cracked when he walked on it.

Hard Rock Returns to Prison from the Hospital for the Criminal Insane

Hard Rock was 'known not to take no shit
From nobody', and he had the scars to prove it:
Split purple lips, lumped ears, welts above
His yellow eyes, and one long scar that cut
Across his temple and plowed through a thick
Canopy of kinky hair.

The WORD was that Hard Rock wasn't a mean nigger
Anymore, that the doctors had bored a hole in his head,
Cut out part of his brain, and shot electricity
Through the rest. When they brought Hard Rock back,
Handcuffed and chained, he was turned loose,
Like a freshly gelded stallion, to try his new status.
And we all waited and watched, like indians at a corral,
To see if the WORD was true.

As we waited we wrapped ourselves in the cloak
Of his exploits: 'Man, the last time, it took eight
Screws to put him in the Hole.' 'Yeah, remember when he
Smacked the captain with his dinner tray?' 'He set
The record for the time in the Hole – 67 straight days!'
'Ol Hard Rock! man, that's one crazy nigger.'
And then the jewel of a myth that Hard Rock had once bit
A screw on the thumb and poisoned him with syphilitic spit.

The testing came, to see if Hard Rock was really tame.
A hillbilly called him a black son of a bitch
And didn't lose his teeth, a screw who knew Hard Rock
From before shook him down and barked in his face.

And Hard Rock did *nothing*. Just grinned and looked silly,
His eyes empty like knot holes in a fence.

And even after we discovered that it took Hard Rock
Exactly 3 minutes to tell you his first name,
We told ourselves that he had just wised up,
Was being cool; but we could not fool ourselves for long,
And we turned away, our eyes on the ground. Crushed.
He had been our Destroyer, the doer of things
We dreamed of doing but could not bring ourselves to do,
The fears of years, like a biting whip,
Had cut grooves too deeply across our backs.

from Peter Grimes

Thus by himself compell'd to live each day,
To wait for certain hours the tide's delay;
At the same times the same dull views to see,
The bounding marsh-bank and the blighted tree;
The water only, when the tides were high,
When low, the mud half-cover'd and half-dry;
The sun-burnt tar that blisters on the planks,
And bank-side stakes in their uneven ranks;
Heaps of entangled weeds that slowly float,
As the tide rolls by the impeded boat.
    When tides were neap, and, in the sultry day,
Through the tall bounding mud-banks made their way,
Which on each side rose swelling, and below
The dark warm flood ran silently and slow;
There anchoring, Peter chose from man to hide,
There hang his head, and view the lazy tide
In its hot slimy channel slowly glide;
Where the small eels that left the deeper way
For the warm shore, within the shallows play;
Where gaping muscles, left upon the mud,
Slope their slow passage to the fallen flood; –
Here dull and hopeless he'd lie down and trace
How sidelong crabs had scrawl'd their crooked race;
Or sadly listen to the tuneless cry
Of fishing gull or clanging golden-eye;
What time the sea-birds to the marsh would come,
And the loud bittern from the bull-rush home,
Gave from the salt-ditch side the bellowing boom:
He nursed the feelings these dull scenes produce,

And loved to stop beside the opening sluice;
Where the small stream, confined in narrow bound,
Ran with a dull, unvaried, sadd'ning sound;
Where all, presented to the eye or ear,
Oppress'd the soul with misery, grief, and fear.

ANTONIO MACHADO

The Ephemeral Past

Habitué of a small-town club, this man
who saw Carancha poised one day
to take the bull,
has a withered skin, hair going grey,
eyes dim with disenchantment, and beneath
the grey moustache, lips bent
in nausea and a look
that's sad – yet sadness it is not
but something more, and less: the void
of the world in the hollow of his head. He still
sports a jacket coloured currant-red
in a three pile velvet, breeches
booted at their extremities and a caramel
Córdoba hat, turned and furbished well.
Three times he inherited, then lost the lot
three times at cards and twice
was widowed. An illegal round of chance
alone will make him brighten
sprawled at the green baize table;
once more the blood begins to flow
as he recollects a gambler's luck
or the afternoon of some torero,
drinks in an episode from the life
of a daring bandit of the road
or the bloody prowess of a knife.
He satirizes with a yawn the government's
reactionary politics and then
predicts the liberals will come to power
again, just as the stork returns to the bell-tower.

[143]

Something of the farmer still, he eyes
the heavens, fears them and at times will sigh
thinking of his olives and, disconsolate,
watches for weather-signs, when rain is late.
For the rest, boredom. Taciturn, hypochondriac,
shut in the Arcadia of the present,
and to his brow
only the movement of the smoke gives now
its look of thought. This man is neither
of yesterday nor tomorrow
but of never. Hispanic stock, he's not
the fruit that grew to ripen or to rot,
but shadow-fruit
from a Spain that did not come to be,
that passed away, yet, dead,
persists to haunt us with a greying head.

Translated by Charles Tomlinson and Henry Gifford

Next Day

Moving from Cheer to Joy, from Joy to All,
I take a box
And add it to my wild rice, my Cornish game hens.
The slacked or shorted, basketed, identical
Food-gathering flocks
Are selves I overlook. Wisdom, said William James,

Is learning what to overlook. And I am wise
If that is wisdom.
Yet somehow, as I buy All from these shelves
And the boy takes it to my station wagon,
What I've become
Troubles me even if I shut my eyes.

When I was young and miserable and pretty
And poor, I'd wish
What all girls wish: to have a husband,
A house and children. Now that I'm old, my wish
Is womanish:
That the boy putting groceries in my car

See me. It bewilders me he doesn't see me.
For so many years
I was good enough to eat: the world looked at me
And its mouth watered. How often they have undressed me,
The eyes of strangers!
And, holding their flesh within my flesh, their vile

Imaginings within my imagining,
I too have taken
The chance of life. Now the boy pats my dog

And we start home. Now I am good.
The last mistaken,
Ecstatic, accidental bliss, the blind

Happiness that, bursting, leaves upon the palm
Some soap and water –
It was so long ago, back in some Gay
Twenties, Nineties, I don't know . . . Today I miss
My lovely daughter
Away at school, my sons away at school,

My husband away at work – I wish for them.
The dog, the maid,
And I go through the sure unvarying days
At home in them. As I look at my life,
I am afraid
Only that it will change, as I am changing:

I am afraid, this morning, of my face.
It looks at me
From the rear-view mirror, with the eyes I hate,
The smile I hate. Its plain, lined look
Of gray discovery
Repeats to me: 'You're old.' That's all, I'm old.

And yet I'm afraid, as I was at the funeral
I went to yesterday.
My friend's cold made-up face, granite among its flowers,
Her undressed, operated-on, dressed body
Were my face and body.
As I think of her I hear her telling me

How young I seem; I *am* exceptional;
I think of all I have.
But really no one is exceptional,

No one has anything, I'm anybody,
I stand beside my grave
Confused with my life, that is commonplace and solitary.

You are Old, Father William

'You are old, Father William,' the young man said,
    'And your hair has become very white;
And yet you incessantly stand on your head –
    Do you think, at your age, it is right?'

'In my youth,' Father William replied to his son,
    'I feared it might injure the brain;
But now that I'm perfectly sure I have none,
    Why, I do it again and again.'

'You are old,' said the youth, 'as I mentioned before,
    And have grown most uncommonly fat;
Yet you turned a back-somersault in at the door –
    Pray, what is the reason of that?'

'In my youth,' said the sage, as he shook his grey locks,
    'I kept all my limbs very supple
By the use of this ointment – one shilling the box –
    Allow me to sell you a couple.'

'You are old,' said the youth, 'and your jaws are too weak
    For anything tougher than suet;
Yet you finished the goose, with the bones and the beak –
    Pray, how did you manage to do it?'

'In my youth,' said his father, 'I took to the law,
    And argued each case with my wife;
And the muscular strength which it gave to my jaw
    Has lasted the rest of my life.'

'You are old,' said the youth; 'one would hardly suppose
    That your eye was as steady as ever;

Yet you balanced an eel on the end of your nose –
  What made you so awfully clever?'

'I have answered three questions, and that is enough,'
  Said his father; 'don't give yourself airs!
Do you think I can listen all day to such stuff?
  Be off, or I'll kick you down stairs!'

JOHN WILMOT, EARL OF ROCHESTER

A Song of a Young Lady to Her Ancient Lover

Ancient person, for whom I
All the flattering youth defy,
Long be it ere thou grow old,
Aching, shaking, crazy, cold;
    But still continue as thou art,
    Ancient person of my heart.

On thy withered lips and dry,
Which like barren furrows lie,
Brooding kisses I will pour
Shall thy youthful [heat] restore
(Such kind showers in autumn fall,
And a second spring recall);
    Nor from thee will ever part,
    Ancient person of my heart.

Thy nobler part, which but to name
In our sex would be counted shame,
By age's frozen grasp possessed,
From [his] ice shall be released,
And soothed by my reviving hand,
In former warmth and vigor stand.
All a lover's wish can reach
For thy joy my love shall teach,
And for thy pleasure shall improve
All that art can add to love.
    Yet still I love thee without art,
    Ancient person of my heart.

An Old Man

At the noisy end of the café, head bent
over the table, an old man sits alone,
a newspaper in front of him.

And in the miserable banality of old age
he thinks how little he enjoyed the years
when he had strength, and wit, and looks.

He knows he's very old now: sees it, feels it.
Yet it seems he was young just yesterday.
The time's gone by so quickly, gone by so quickly.

And he thinks how Discretion fooled him,
how he always believed, so stupidly,
that cheat who said: 'Tomorrow. You have plenty of time.'

He remembers impulses bridled, the joy
he sacrificed. Every chance he lost
now mocks his brainless prudence.

But so much thinking, so much remembering
makes the old man dizzy. He falls asleep,
his head resting on the café table.

translated from the Greek by Edmund Keeley and Philip Sherrard

To an Old Lady

Ripeness is all; her in her cooling planet
Revere; do not presume to think her wasted.
Project her no projectile, plan nor man it;
Gods cool in turn, by the sun long outlasted.

Our earth alone given no name of god
Gives, too, no hold for such a leap to aid her;
Landing, you break some palace and seem odd;
Bees sting their need, the keeper's queen invader.

No, to your telescope; spy out the land;
Watch while her ritual is still to see,
Still stand her temples emptying in the sand
Whose waves o'erthrew their crumbled tracery;

Still stand uncalled-on her soul's appanage;
Much social detail whose successor fades,
Wit used to run a house and to play Bridge,
And tragic fervour, to dismiss her maids.

Years her precession do not throw from gear.
She reads a compass certain of her pole;
Confident, finds no confines on her sphere,
Whose failing crops are in her sole control.

Stars how much further from me fill my night.
Strange that she too should be inaccessible,
Who shares my sun. He curtains her from sight,
And but in darkness is she visible.

Wellingtonia

From his armchair in the home counties
grandpa followed our Asian journeys
with an atlas of the world and supplement
of postcards, hasty and irregular,
from Delhi, Cochin, the southern tip of India.
He plotted the route with eccentric care
as if he'd travelled it. But when I came back
taller, with the deferent condescension
of the barely adult, he missed the boy
back in the kitchen playing Snap with Ada.

Ada ruled the larder. My life was pale yellow.
There was bread and butter, Gentleman's Relish,
a drawer of knives, a row of yellow bells,
two sisters and a blue Wellingtonia.
We gathered up dead needles by the handful,
but the tree renews them, said grandpa,
full of facts and detail. In the war
he drilled his soldiers on the tennis lawn
or so my mother said. I liked to linger
in the shadow of a pine green corridor.

I felt the velvet drapes and smelt the turpentine
but loathed the girlish shoes I had to pose in.
Granny was an upstairs painter, her studio
an attic. Downstairs was dark, the conversation
social: families, marriages, property, sport.
Once under drugs, granny rose from her ground-floor
death bed and with uncontrollable strength
began to mount the stairs. She was found

in the small hours, more than half-way up,
scrabbling at a window as if for air.

She spurned her nurses, dreading helplessness.
Prodigal of flowers, her lacquered garlands
live with us on tables, beds and chairs.
A morning fire below the smoky mirror,
a mixture of lights, tonic in a glass
can reassemble her to me. The Wellingtonia
dropped its skirts of branch almost to the lawn,
extinguishing the grown-up room in shadow.
The turn in the corridor was always dark.
Grandpa packed her portrait and moved on.

Later, he found he shared an interest
with his otherwise, disappointing grandson
– bookish, secretive, no good at sports –
and that was pipe-smoking. We would light up
together, a rosewood briar and a meerschaum,
breathe in with the little pop of fishes,
tamp the tobacco down and move off slowly
crunching round the gravel drive. I still
have the last of the Three Nuns and cleaners.
My other achievement was a motorcycle.

Uncle Stan

Here's Uncle Stan, his hair a comber, slick
In his Sundays, buttoning a laugh;
Gazing, sweet-chestnut eyed, out of a thick
Ship's biscuit of a studio photograph.
He's Uncle Stan, the darling of our clan,
Throttled by celluloid: the slow-worm thin
Tie, the dandy's rose, Kirk Douglas chin
Hatched on the card in various shades of tan.

He died when I was in my pram; became
The hero of my child's mythology.
Youngest of seven, gave six of us his name
If not his looks, and gradually he
Was Ulysses, Jack Marvel, Amyas Leigh.
Before the Kaiser's war, crossed the grave sea
And to my mother wrote home forest tales
In Church School script of bears and waterfalls.

I heard, a hundred times, of how and when
The blacksmith came and nipped off every curl
('So that he don't look too much like a girl')
And how Stan tried to stick them on again.
As quavering children, how they dragged to feed
The thudding pig; balanced on the sty-beams,
Hurled bucket, peelings on its pitching head –
Fled, twice a day, from its enormous screams.

I watched the tears jerk on my mother's cheek
For his birth day; and gently she would speak
Of how time never told the way to quell
The brisk pain of their whistle-stop farewell:

A London train paused in the winter-bleak
Of Teignmouth. To his older friend said, 'Take
Good care of him.' Sensed, from a hedging eye,
All that was said when neither made reply.
I look at the last photograph. He stands
In wrinkled khaki, firm as Hercules,
Pillars of legs apart, and in his hands
A cane; defying the cold lens to ease
Forward an inch. Here's Uncle Stan, still game,
As Private, 1st Canadians, trimmed for war.
Died at Prince Rupert, B. C. And whose name
Lives on, in confident brass, for evermore.

That's all I know of Uncle Stan. Those who
Could tell the rest are flakes of ash, lie deep
As Cornish tin, or flatfish. 'Sweet as dew,'
They said. Yet – what else made them keep
His memory fresh as a young tree? Perhaps
The lure of eyes, quick with large love, is clue
To what I'll never know, and the bruised maps
Of other hearts will never lead me to.
He might have been a farmer; swallowed mud
At Vimy, Cambrai; smiling, have rehearsed
To us the silent history of his blood:
But a Canadian winter got him first.

To Eugene Lambe in Heaven

It's after closing-time on a winter's night
in Smoky Joe's café a generation ago –
rain and smoke, and the tables are packed tight
with drunken students kicking up a racket,
exchanging insults, looking for a fight
since there's nothing to do and nowhere else to go;
and the sad Italians (parents, daughter, son)
who own the place and serve these savages
of the harsh north their chips and sausages
look up and grin with relief as you come in,
their baffled faces lighting up at once
at your quaint 'whisker' and velvet smoking-jacket,
your manner that of an exiled Stuart prince
transfiguring tedium . . . Next year you appeared
in the same gear and spread Tolstoyan beard,
our ginger man, in Trinity's front square
you called the 'playground' once; and it was here
in pub and flat you formed the character
we came to love, colloquial yet ornate,
one of those perfect writers who never write,
a student of manners and conversation straight
from the pages of Castiglione or Baudelaire:
'a form of pride rare in this generation,
stoical, spiritual even, resistant to the trite;
the Protestant countries lack gallantry and devotion . . .'
Not that you read much, you had no need to read
so flunked your courses; destined for the law
took up, instead, interior decoration,
installing yourself wherever the calling led

and awaiting the 'rush of gold' you never saw.
There you were, in the fine house of a friend,
a citrous gin or herbal tea to hand,
young women in attendance, an abashed host constrained
to listen patiently while you explained
the iniquity of ownership; for you had no ambition
save for the moment, of will-power not a whit
since nothing could measure up to your idea of it.
Dublin in the '60s! – Golden days
of folk revival, tin whistle and *bodhrán*,
ecology, yin and yang, CND, late-century blues,
Gandolf's Garden, *Bananas* and *Peace News*;
then London, Covent Garden, quit the booze
but dreamed the hashish poem on opera nights,
De Quincey's 'infinite ecstasies, infinite repose',
while living above the market unknown to the old fogies
ensconced in the Garrick with their port and stogies
and the hacks in the Coach & Horses, *laudatores*
temporis acti, unregenerate Tories
shut out for ever from your generous insights.
At a time of drag and Pop Art, hair and clothes,
Beardsley prints, floral design and rainbow hues,
of Quant and Biba, Shrimpton and Twiggy, lurid tights,
gratuitous gesture, instant celebrity, insolent pose,
yours was a sociable life but a lonely one,
your castle of indolence a monastic den
where you sat up late to contemplate the din
of Leicester Square, Long Acre and Drury Lane,
vocations entertained but never followed through.
A job, a house, a car, perhaps a wife,
financial panic, the 'normal' sort of life
so many know, such things were not for you
who made the great refusal but remained

philosophical with your dwindling flow of visitors,
chivalrous with women, ceremonious with waiters,
noble in exile, tragic in the end,
and died dancing . . . But hip went out of fashion
in an age of sado-monetarism, and the game
now is to the 'oeconomists and calculators' –
the new harshness must have wounded you to the heart.
We always knew you had too big a heart,
we always knew about the heart condition
you nursed with a vegetarian regime
of rice and nuts. You were a saint and hero
to the young men and girls we used to know
once in the golden age; and now it's closing-time
in the condemned playgrounds that you loved, Eugene,
in Davy Byrne's and Smoky Joe's. The scene
is draggy now in these final days, and with
everyone famous for fifteen minutes, few
survive except those, like you, the stuff of myth.
Oft in the stilly night I remember our wasted youth.

Danny

One night a score of Erris men,
A score I'm told and nine,
Said, 'We'll get shut of Danny's noise
Of girls and widows dyin'.

'There's not his like from Binghamstown
To Boyle and Ballycroy,
At playing hell on decent girls,
At beating man and boy.

'He's left two pairs of female twins
Beyond in Killacreest,
And twice in Crossmolina fair
He's struck the parish priest.

'But we'll come round him in the night
A mile beyond the Mullet;
Ten will quench his bloody eyes,
And ten will choke his gullet.'

It wasn't long till Danny came,
From Bangor making way,
And he was damning moon and stars
And whistling grand and gay.

Till in a gap of hazel glen –
And not a hare in sight –
Out lepped the nine-and-twenty lads
Along his left and right.

Then Danny smashed the nose on Byrne,
He split the lips on three,

And bit across the right-hand thumb
On one Red Shawn Magee.

But seven tripped him up behind,
And seven kicked before,
And seven squeezed around his throat
Till Danny kicked no more.

Then some destroyed him with their heels,
Some tramped him in the mud,
Some stole his purse and timber pipe,
And some washed off his blood.

              *

And when you're walking out the way
From Bangor to Belmullet,
You'll see a flat cross on a stone,
Where men choked Danny's gullet.

A . B . (BANJO) PATERSON

How M'Ginnis Went Missing

Let us cease our idle chatter,
　Let the tears bedew our cheek,
For a man from Tallangatta
　Has been missing for a week.

Where the roaring flooded Murray
　Covered all the lower land,
There he started in a hurry,
　With a bottle in his hand.

And his fate is hid for ever,
　But the public seem to think
That he slumbered by the river,
　'Neath the influence of drink.

And they scarcely seem to wonder
　That the river, wide and deep,
Never woke him with its thunder,
　Never stirred him in his sleep.

As the crashing logs came sweeping,
　And their tumult filled the air,
Then M'Ginnis murmured, sleeping,
　''Tis a wake in ould Kildare.'

So the river rose and found him
　Sleeping softly by the stream,
And the cruel waters drowned him
　Ere he wakened from his dream.

And the blossom-tufted wattle,
  Blooming brightly on the lea,
Saw M'Ginnis and the bottle
  Going drifting out to sea.

Tommy

I went into a public-'ouse to get a pint o' beer,
The publican 'e up an' sez, 'We serve no red-coats 'ere.'
The girls be'ind the bar they laughed and giggled fit to die,
I outs into the street again, an' to myself sez I:
    Oh, it's Tommy this, an' Tommy that, an' 'Tommy, go away';
    But it's 'Thank you, Mister Atkins,' when the band begins
      to play –
    The band begins to play, my boys, the band begins to play,
    Oh, it's 'Thank you, Mister Atkins,' when the band begins
      to play.

I went into a theatre as sober as could be,
They gave a drunk civilian room, but 'adn't none for me;
They sent me to the gallery or round the music-'alls,
But when it comes to fightin', Lord! they'll shove me in the
      stalls!
    For it's Tommy this, an' Tommy that, an' 'Tommy, wait
      outside';
    But it's 'Special train for Atkins' when the trooper's on
      the tide –
    The troopship's on the tide, my boys, the troopship's on
      the tide,
    Oh, it's 'Special train for Atkins' when the trooper's on
      the tide.

Yes, makin' mock o' uniforms that guard you while you sleep
Is cheaper than them uniforms, an' they're starvation cheap;
An' hustlin' drunken soldiers when they're goin' large a bit
Is five times better business than paradin' in full kit.

Then it's Tommy this, an' Tommy that, an' 'Tommy, 'ow's
    yer soul?'
But it's 'Thin red line of 'eroes' when the drums begin to roll,
The drums begin to roll, my boys, the drums begin to roll,
Oh, it's 'Thin red line of 'eroes' when the drums begin to roll.

We aren't no thin red 'eroes, nor we aren't no blackguards too,
But single men in barricks, most remarkable like you;
An' if sometimes our conduck isn't all your fancy paints,
Why, single men in barricks don't grow into plaster saints;
    While it's Tommy this, an' Tommy that, an' 'Tommy, fall
        be'ind,'
    But it's 'Please to walk in front, sir,' when there's trouble
        in the wind –
    There's trouble in the wind, my boys, there's trouble in
        the wind,
    Oh, it's 'Please to walk in front, sir,' when there's trouble
        in the wind.

You talk o' better food for us, an' schools, an' fires, an' all:
We'll wait for extry rations if you treat us rational.
Don't mess about the cook-room slops, but prove it to our face
The Widow's Uniform is not the soldier-man's disgrace.
    For it's Tommy this, an' Tommy that, an' 'Chuck him out,
        the brute!'
    But it's 'Saviour of 'is country' when the guns begin to
        shoot;
    An' it's Tommy this, an' Tommy that, an' anything you
        please;
    An' Tommy ain't a bloomin' fool – you bet that Tommy sees!

An Elegy

Friend, whose unnatural early death
In this year's cold, chaotic Spring
Is like a clumsy wound that will not heal:
What can I say to you, now that your ears
Are stoppered-up with distant soil?
Perhaps to speak at all is false; more true
Simply to sit at times alone and dumb
And with most pure intensity of thought
And concentrated inmost feeling, reach
Towards your shadow on the years' crumbling wall.

I'll say not any word in praise or blame
Of what you ended with the mere turn of a tap;
Nor to explain, deplore not yet exploit
The latent pathos of your living years –
Hurried, confused and unfulfilled –
That were the shiftless years of both our youths
Spent in the monstrous mountain-shadow of
Catastrophe that chilled you to the bone:
The certain imminence of which always pursued
You from your heritage of fields and sun . . .

I see your face in hostile sunlight, eyes
Wrinkled against its glare, behind the glass
Of a car's windscreen, while you seek to lose
Yourself in swift devouring of white roads
Unwinding across Europe or America;
Taciturn at the wheel, wrapped in a blaze
Of restlessness that no fresh scene can quench;
In cities of brief sojourn that you pass

Through in your quest for respite, heavy drink
Alone enabling you to bear each hotel night.

Sex, Art and Politics: those poor
Expedients! You tried them each in turn,
With the wry inward smile of one resigned
To join in every complicated game
Adults affect to play. Yet girls you found
So prone to sentiment's corruptions; and the joy
Of sensual satisfaction seemed so brief, and left
Only new need. It proved hard to remain
Convinced of the World's efficacity; or even quite
Certain of World-Salvation through 'the Party Line' . . .

Cased in the careful armour that you wore
Of wit and nonchalance, through which
Few quizzed the concealed countenance of fear
You waited daily for the sky to fall;
At moments wholly panic-stricken by
A sense of stifling in your brittle shell;
Seeing the world's damnation week by week
Grow more and more inevitable; till
The conflagration broke out with a roar,
And from those flames you fled through whirling smoke,

To end at last in bankrupt exile in
That sordid city, scene of *Ulysses*; and there,
While War sowed all the lands with violent graves,
You finally succumbed to a black, wild
Incomprehensibility of fate that none could share . . .
Yet even in your obscure death I see
The secret candour of that lonely child

Who, lost in the storm-shaken castle-park,
Astride his crippled mastiff's back was borne
Slowly away into the utmost dark.

Waring

I

I

What's become of Waring
Since he gave us all the slip,
Chose land-travel or seafaring,
Boots and chest or staff and scrip,
Rather than pace up and down
Any longer London town?

II

Who'd have guessed it from his lip
Or his brow's accustomed bearing,
On the night he thus took ship
Or started landward? – little caring
For us, it seems, who supped together
(Friends of his too, I remember)
And walked home thro' the merry weather,
The snowiest in all December.
I left his arm that night myself
For what's-his-name's, the new prose-poet
Who wrote the book there, on the shelf –
How, forsooth, was I to know it
If Waring meant to glide away
Like a ghost at break of day?
Never looked he half so gay!

He was prouder than the devil:
How he must have cursed our revel!
Ay and many other meetings,
Indoor visits, outdoor greetings,
As up and down he paced this London,
With no work done, but great works undone.
Where scarce twenty knew his name.
Why not, then, have earlier spoken,
Written, bustled? Who's to blame
If your silence kept unbroken?
'True, but there were sundry jottings,
'Stray-leaves, fragments, blurrs and blottings,
'Certain first steps were achieved
'Already which' – (is that your meaning?)
'Had well borne out whoe'er believed
'In more to come!' But who goes gleaning
Hedgeside chance-blades, while full-sheaved
Stand cornfields by him? Pride, o'erweening
Pride alone, puts forth such claims
O'er the day's distinguished names.

IV

Meantime, how much I loved him,
I find out now I've lost him.
I who cared not if I moved him,
Who could so carelessly accost him,
Henceforth never shall get free
Of his ghostly company,
His eyes that just a little wink
As deep I go into the merit
Of this and that distinguished spirit –

His cheeks' raised colour, soon to sink,
As long I dwell on some stupendous
And tremendous (Heaven defend us!)
Monstr'-inform'-ingens-horrend-ous
Demoniaco-seraphic
Penman's latest piece of graphic.
Nay, my very wrist grows warm
With his dragging weight of arm.
E'en so, swimmingly appears,
Through one's after-supper musings,
Some lost lady of old years
With her beauteous vain endeavour
And goodness unrepaid as ever;
The face, accustomed to refusings,
We, puppies that we were . . . Oh never
Surely, nice of conscience, scrupled
Being aught like false, forsooth, to?
Telling aught but honest truth to?
What a sin, had we centupled
Its possessor's grace and sweetness!
No! she heard in its completeness
Truth, for truth's a weighty matter,
And, truth at issue, we can't flatter!
Well, 't is done with; she's exempt
From damning us thro' such a sally;
And so she glides, as down a valley,
Taking up with her contempt,
Past our reach; and in, the flowers
Shut her unregarded hours.

V

Oh, could I have him back once more,
This Waring, but one half-day more!

Back, with the quiet face of yore,
So hungry for acknowledgment
Like mine! I'd fool him to his bent.
Feed, should not he, to heart's content?
I'd say, 'to only have conceived,
'Planned your great works, apart from progress,
'Surpasses little works achieved!'
I'd lie so, I should be believed.
I'd make such havoc of the claims
Of the day's distinguished names
To feast him with, as feasts an ogress
Her feverish sharp-toothed gold-crowned child!
Or as one feasts a creature rarely
Captured here, unreconciled
To capture; and completely gives
Its pettish humours license, barely
Requiring that it lives.

VI

Ichabod, Ichabod,
The glory is departed!
Travels Waring East away?
Who, of knowledge, by hearsay,
Reports a man upstarted
Somewhere as a god,
Hordes grown European-hearted,
Millions of the wild made tame
On a sudden at his fame?
In Vishnu-land what Avatar?
Or who in Moscow, toward the Czar,
With the demurest of footfalls
Over the Kremlin's pavement bright
With serpentine and syenite,

Steps, with five other Generals
That simultaneously take snuff,
For each to have pretext enough
And kerchiefwise unfold his sash
Which, softness' self, is yet the stuff
To hold fast where a steel chain snaps,
And leave the grand white neck no gash?
Waring in Moscow, to those rough
Cold northern natures borne perhaps,
Like the lambwhite maiden dear
From the circle of mute kings
Unable to repress the tear,
Each as his sceptre down he flings,
To Dian's fane at Taurica,
Where now a captive priestess, she alway
Mingles her tender grave Hellenic speech
With theirs, tuned to the hailstone-beaten beach
As pours some pigeon, from the myrrhy lands
Rapt by the whirlblast to fierce Scythian strands
Where breed the swallows, her melodious cry
Amid their barbarous twitter!
In Russia? Never! Spain was fitter!
Ay, most likely 't is in Spain
That we and Waring meet again
Now, while he turns down that cool narrow lane
Into the blackness, out of grave Madrid
All fire and shine, abrupt as when there's slid
Its stiff gold blazing pall
From some black coffin-lid.
Or, best of all,
I love to think
The leaving us was just a feint;
Back here to London did he slink,

And now works on without a wink
Of sleep, and we are on the brink
Of something great in fresco-paint:
Some garret's ceiling, walls and floor,
Up and down and o'er and o'er
He splashes, as none splashed before
Since great Caldara Polidore.
Or Music means this land of ours
Some favour yet, to pity won
By Purcell from his Rosy Bowers, –
'Give me my so-long promised son,
'Let Waring end what I begun!'
Then down he creeps and out he steals
Only when the night conceals
His face; in Kent 't is cherry-time,
Or hops are picking: or at prime
Of March he wanders as, too happy,
Years ago when he was young,
Some mild eve when woods grew sappy
And the early moths had sprung
To life from many a trembling sheath
Woven the warm boughs beneath;
While small birds said to themselves
What should soon be actual song,
And young gnats, by tens and twelves,
Made as if they were the throng
That crowd around and carry aloft
The sound they have nursed, so sweet and pure,
Out of a myriad noises soft,
Into a tone that can endure
Amid the noise of a July noon
When all God's creatures crave their boon,
All at once and all in tune,

And get it, happy as Waring then,
Having first within his ken
What a man might do with men:
And far too glad, in the even-glow,
To mix with the world he meant to take
Into his hand, he told you, so –
And out of it his world to make,
To contract and to expand
As he shut or oped his hand.
Oh Waring, what's to really be?
A clear stage and a crowd to see!
Some Garrick, say, out shall not he
The heart of Hamlet's mystery pluck?
Or, where most unclean beasts are rife,
Some Junius – am I right? – shall tuck
His sleeve, and forth with flaying-knife!
Some Chatterton shall have the luck
Of calling Rowley into life!
Some one shall somehow run a muck
With this old world for want of strife
Sound asleep. Contrive, contrive
To rouse us, Waring! Who's alive?
Our men scarce seem in earnest now.
Distinguished names! – but 't is, somehow,
As if they played at being names
Still more distinguished, like the games
Of children. Turn our sport to earnest
With a visage of the sternest!
Bring the real times back, confessed
Still better than our very best!

I

'When I last saw Waring ...'
(How all turned to him who spoke!
You saw Waring? Truth or joke?
In land-travel or sea-faring?)

II

'We were sailing by Triest
'Where a day or two we harboured:
'A sunset was in the West,
'When, looking over the vessel's side,
'One of our company espied
'A sudden speck to larboard.
'And as a sea-duck flies and swims
'At once, so came the light craft up,
'With its sole lateen sail that trims
'And turns (the water round its rims
'Dancing, as round a sinking cup)
'And by us like a fish it curled,
'And drew itself up close beside,
'Its great sail on the instant furled,
'And o'er its thwarts a shrill voice cried,
'(A neck as bronzed as a Lascar's)
' "Buy wine of us, you English Brig?
' "Or fruit, tobacco and cigars?
' "A pilot for you to Triest?
' "Without one, look you ne'er so big,
' "They'll never let you up the bay!
' "We natives should know best."
'I turned, and "just those fellows' way,"

'Our captain said, "The 'long-shore thieves
' "Are laughing at us in their sleeves."

III

'In truth, the boy leaned laughing back;
'And one, half-hidden by his side
'Under the furled sail, soon I spied,
'With great grass hat and kerchief black,
'Who looked up with his kingly throat,
'Said somewhat, while the other shook
'His hair back from his eyes to look
'Their longest at us; then the boat,
'I know not how, turned sharply round,
'Laying her whole side on the sea
'As a leaping fish does; from the lee
'Into the weather, cut somehow
'Her sparkling path beneath our bow
'And so went off, as with a bound,
'Into the rosy and golden half
'O' the sky, to overtake the sun
'And reach the shore, like the sea-calf
'Its singing cave; yet I caught one
'Glance ere away the boat quite passed,
'And neither time nor toil could mar
'Those features: so I saw the last
'Of Waring!' – You? Oh, never star
Was lost here but it rose afar!
Look East, where whole new thousands are!
In Vishnu-land what Avatar?

JOHN FULLER

The Ballad of Lord Timbal

Beside a flashing gramophone
And the latest magazines
Lord Timbal watched the chequered sea,
Its curling whites and greens.

Stretched round him on the silver sand
On turquoise towels lay
The last guests at his villa
Spending their last day.

Lord Timbal was a gentleman
And of the richest kind:
He bought his life with little cheques
And every cheque was signed.

And every cheque was handsome
And every cheque was met,
And each of his acquaintances
Was in Lord Timbal's debt.

Beneath a cup-shaped rock he sat,
His wristwatch lattice gold.
He did not buy love with his cheques
For love could not be sold.

He watched each pair of faces
That touched each other there,
And he sat unknown among them,
Among the bronzed and fair.

He slipped on his dark glasses,
Mirrors in precious stone:

He saw their puzzled faces,
But they only saw their own.

And in these one-way glasses
He heard their whispered words
As they huddled on his private beach
Like migrating birds:

'Why does he live alone here
At the age of twenty-three,
With his face as pale as a ceiling
And his hair as wild as the sea?'

'Who *is* he, our host, with his empty chair
And the presents on our plate?'
'Will he wave to us at the station?'
'Hurry or we'll be late.'

His servant drove ten hampers down,
Bursting with veal and hock,
And the train was out and the party gone
Like a glimpse of a summer frock.

Lord Timbal stayed behind alone,
And, like a gay reproof,
He saw the puffs of train smoke drift
Beyond the villa's roof.

He went from hut to bathing hut,
Frowning at what he saw,
And at a trace of woman's scent
He turned and slammed the door.

He entered all the bedrooms
And opened all the drawers,

And the sea's roar in his head became
Ironical applause:

'O honest player, play your hand,
Harden your honest face.
The ace is low in the game of life,
And you've drawn the ace.'

His man came back from the station
And stood at the foot of the stair.
The young lord went to the stairhead
And saw him standing there.

Lord Timbal looked down strangely
With his fingers at his cheek,
Parting his cold romantic lips
As if he meant to speak.

Amused, the servant turned away,
Began to pick his nails,
And Lord Timbal came down the staircase
Grasping both the rails.

He looked into his servant's eye
As if it held some clue.
And there he read the deepest scorn,
But a little pity, too:

'You've never really loved, nor will.
You love yourself, your past.
You are unhappy. You will die.
Need you ask?'

The cool stare sinking in his heart
As the sea receives a stone,

He opened the french windows
And strolled out on his own.

The bay was clearing its green throat,
The sea sniffed at the rocks,
A sudden wind rose up and blew
Lord Timbal's thinning locks.

He looked up to the terrace
And saw his servant there,
Wrapping away the cutlery
With a fatal, final air.

Lord Timbal now was fearless.
Grimly he clambered on
His cream and brass expensive yacht
And sailed off like a swan.

He sailed into a mid-sea storm
And there without a sound
The swollen sails exploded
And Lord Timbal was drowned.

'Lord Timbal is dead, Lord Timbal is dead,'
A wind to the people roared.
But they turned and sadly whispered:
'Lucky for that poor lord.

'Idle he died as idle lived,
Empty the life he lead.
He spent his pounds like bullets
And his love like lead.'

A few crept from their dwellings
And then came more, and more.

With faces lined and heavy,
They waited on the shore.

They watched the ocean rise and fall
With the glow of the fishing floats
And their eyes stared long at the water
As the men dragged down their boats.

His body was slowly borne along
On the stretchers of the sea,
And all the drums of the Spanish coast
Beat in sympathy.

LOUIS MACNIECE

Suicide

He had fought for the wrong causes,
Had married the wrong wife,
Had invested rashly, had lost
His health and his reputation,
His fortune and his looks.

Who in his youth had gone
Walking on the crown of the road
Under delectable trees
And over irresponsible moors
To find the rainbow's end;

And was now, at forty-nine,
Living in a half-timbered
Cottage with a pale
Mistress and some gardening
Books and a life of Napoleon.

When she left him he took
The shears and clipped the hedge
And then taking his rifle
As if for duck went out
Walking on the crown of the road.

An Epitaph on M. H.

In this cold monument lies one,
That I knew who has lain upon,
The happier He: her sight would charm,
And touch have kept King David warm.
Lovely, as is the dawning East,
Was this marble's frozen guest;
As soft, and snowy, as that down
Adorns the blow-ball's frizzled crown;
As straight and slender as the crest,
Or antlet of the one-beam'd beast;
Pleasant as th' odorous month of May:
As glorious, and as light as day.

Whom I admir'd, as soon as knew,
And now her memory pursue
With such a superstitious lust,
That I could fumble with her dust.

She all perfections had, and more,
Tempting, as if design'd a whore,
For so she was; and since there are
Such, I could wish them all as fair.

Pretty she was, and young, and wise,
And in her calling so precise,
That industry had made her prove
The sucking school-mistress of love:
And Death, ambitious to become
Her pupil, left his ghastly home,
And, seeing how we us'd her here,
The raw-boned rascal ravish'd her.

Who, pretty soul, resign'd her breath,
To seek new lechery in Death.

On the Death of Dr Robert Levet

Condemn'd to hope's delusive mine,
    As on we toil from day to day,
By sudden blasts, or slow decline,
    Our social comforts drop away.

Well tried through many a varying year,
    See LEVET to the grave descend;
Officious, innocent, sincere,
    Of ev'ry friendless name the friend.

Yet still he fills affection's eye,
    Obscurely wise, and coarsely kind;
Nor, letter'd arrogance, deny
    Thy praise to merit unrefin'd.

When fainting nature call'd for aid,
    And hov'ring death prepar'd the blow,
His vig'rous remedy display'd
    The power of art without the show.

In misery's darkest caverns known,
    His useful care was ever nigh,
Where hopeless anguish pour'd his groan,
    And lonely want retir'd to die.

No summons mock'd by chill delay,
    No petty gain disdain'd by pride,
The modest wants of ev'ry day
    The toil of ev'ry day supplied.

His virtues walk'd their narrow round,
    Nor made a pause, nor left a void;

And sure th' Eternal Master found
    The single talent well employ'd.

The busy day, the peaceful night,
    Unfelt, uncounted, glided by;
His frame was firm, his powers were bright,
    Tho' now his eightieth year was nigh.

Then with no throbbing fiery pain,
    No cold gradations of decay,
Death broke at once the vital chain,
    And free'd his soul the nearest way.

On the Death of Mr William Harvey

It was a dismal and a fearful night,
Scarce could the morn drive on the unwilling light,
When Sleep, Death's image, left my troubled breast
 By something liker Death possest.
My eyes with tears did uncommanded flow,
 And on my soul hung the dull weight
 Of some intolerable fate.
What bell was that? Ah me! too much I know.

My sweet companion, and my gentle peer,
Why hast thou left me thus unkindly here,
Thy end forever, and my life to moan?
 O thou hast left me all alone!
Thy soul and body, when death's agony
 Besieged around thy noble heart,
 Did not with more reluctance part
Than I, my dearest Friend, do part from thee.

My dearest Friend, would I had died for thee!
Life and this world henceforth will tedious be.
Nor shall I know hereafter what to do
 If once my griefs prove tedious too.
Silent and sad I walk about all day,
 As sullen ghosts stalk speechless by
 Where their hid treasures lie;
Alas, my treasure's gone, why do I stay?

He was my friend, the truest friend on earth;
A strong and mighty influence joined our birth.
Nor did we envy the most sounding name
 By Friendship given of old to Fame.

None but his brethren he, and sisters, knew
   Whom the kind youth preferred to me;
   And even in that we did agree,
For much above myself I loved them too.

Say, for you saw us, ye immortal lights,
How oft unwearied have we spent the nights,
Till the Ledaean stars, so famed for love,
   Wondered at us from above?
We spent them not in toys, in lusts, or wine,
   But search of deep Philosophy,
   Wit, Eloquence, and Poetry,
Arts which I loved, for they, my Friend, were thine.

Ye fields of Cambridge, our dear Cambridge, say,
Have ye not seen us walking every day?
Was there a tree about which did not know
   The love betwixt us two?
Henceforth, ye gentle trees, forever fade;
   Or your sad branches thicker join
   And into darksome shades combine,
Dark as the grave wherein my friend is laid. . . .

The Unknown Citizen

(To JS/07/M/378)
This Marble Monument
Is Erected by the State

He was found by the Bureau of Statistics to be
One against whom there was no official complaint,
And all the reports on his conduct agree
That, in the modern sense of an old-fashioned word, he was
    a saint,
For in everything he did he served the Greater Community.
Except for the War till the day he retired
He worked in a factory and never got fired,
But satisfied his employers, Fudge Motors Inc.
Yet he wasn't a scab or odd in his views,
For his Union reports that he paid his dues,
(Our report on his Union shows it was sound)
And our Social Psychology workers found
That he was popular with his mates and liked a drink.
The Press are convinced that he bought a paper every day
And that his reactions to advertisements were normal in
    every way.
Policies taken out in his name prove that he was fully
    insured,
And his Health-card shows he was once in hospital but left
    it cured.
Both Producers Research and High-Grade Living declare
He was fully sensible to the advantages of the Instalment
    Plan
And had everything necessary to the Modern Man,
A phonograph, a radio, a car and a frigidaire.

Our researchers into Public Opinion are content
That he held the proper opinions for the time of year;
When there was peace, he was for peace; when there was
   war, he went.
He was married and added five children to the population,
Which our Eugenist says was the right number for a parent
   of his generation,
And our teachers report that he never interfered with their
   education.
Was he free? Was he happy? The question is absurd:
Had anything been wrong, we should certainly have heard.

THOMAS HARDY

The Self-Unseeing

Here is the ancient floor,
Footworn and hollowed and thin,
Here was the former door
Where the dead feet walked in.

She sat here in her chair,
Smiling into the fire;
He who played stood there,
Bowing it higher and higher.

Childlike, I danced in a dream;
Blessings emblazoned that day;
Everything glowed with a gleam;
Yet we were looking away!

VALÉRY LARBAUD

The Old Station at Cahors

Traveller! Cosmopolitan! but now
Neglected, retired, put out to grass.
Standing back a little from the line,
Your old rose-pink among the miracles of morning,
With your useless canopy
You stretch your empty platform in the sun
(The platform that was swept, once,
By the great express-trains' swirling skirts of air),
Your silent platform at the edge of a meadow,
The doors of the waiting-room closed for ever,
Their shutters cracked and blistered by the heat of summer . . .
O station, who have witnessed so many farewell scenes,
So many departures and returnings,
Station, a great door open to the lovely immensity
Of the Earth, somewhere on which divine happiness,
Like an unexpected, dazzling thing, must be;
Meanwhile you rest and you taste the seasons
Which bring back the breeze or the sun, and your stones
Feel the cold lightning of the lizards; and the teasing
Of the wind's light fingers in the grass where the rails
Run, red and roughened with rust,
Is your only distraction.
The throbbing of the trains no longer caresses you:
They pass by in the distance without stopping on your lawn,
And leave you to your bucolic peace, O station quiet at last
In the pure heart of France.

NEIL RENNIE

Now Read On

Underneath a Mazda bulb sits Coconut Joe,
head buried in *Tracy chez les coupeurs de têtes*,
having an idea, brilliantly seeing why
the quonset huts where Tracy sang went slowly down,
gurgling, off Million Dollar Point: 'Joe, Joe,
Coconut Joe, walks around like an NCO.'

Acknowledgements

I would like to thank Anthony Astbury for the benefit of his wide reading and tireless photocopying, also James Campbell for suggesting William Dunbar's 'Of Ane Blak-Moir' and Neil Rennie for 'Absolon' from *The Miller's Tale*.

W. H. AUDEN, 'Who's Who', copyright © 1937 and renewed 1965 by W. H. Auden; 'The Unknown Citizen' copyright © 1940 and renewed 1968 by W. H. Auden; 'Epitaph on a Tyrant', copyright © 1940 and renewed 1968 by W. H. Auden; 'Edward Lear' copyright © 1940 and renewed 1968 by W. H. Auden from W. H. Auden: *Collected Poems* by W. H. Auden. Used in Canada by permission of Random House, Inc, and in the rest of the British Commonwealth by permission of Faber and Faber Ltd. PATRICIA BEER, from *Collected Poems*, published by Carcanet Press, 1988, reprinted by permission of the publisher. JOHN BETJEMEN, from *Collected Poems*, published by John Murray (Publishers) Ltd, 1979. ELIZABETH BISHOP, from *The Complete Poems: 1927–1979*. Copyright © 1979, 1983 by Alice Helen Methfessel, reprinted by permission of Farrar Straus and Giroux, LLC. CHARLES BUKOWSKI, from *Septuagenarian Stew Stories and Poems*, published by Airlift Book Co. and Black Sparrow Press. RAYMOND CARVER, FROM *Collected Poems*, published by Harvill Press. CHARLES CAUSLEY, from *Collected Poems 1951–2000*, published by Macmillan, reprinted by permission of David Higham Associates. C. P. CAVAFY, 'An Old Man' by permission of Christopher Reid. NOËL COWARD, from *Not Yet the Dodo*, published by Doubleday, 1967. LAWRENCE DURRELL, from *Collected Poems*, published by Faber and Faber Ltd. T. S. ELIOT, from *Inventions of the March Hare* and *Collected Poems 1909–1962*, published by Faber and Faber Ltd. WILLIAM EMPSON, from *A Collection of Poems*, published by Hogarth Press, used by permission Lady Empson and The Random House Group Limited. D. J. ENRIGHT, 'Dreaming in the Shanghai Restaurant' first published by Carcanet Press and reprinted by permission of Watson, Little Ltd licensing agents. JAMES FENTON, from *The Memory of War*, by permission of the Peters Fraser and Dunlop Group Ltd. ROBERT FROST, from *The Poetry of Robert Frost* edited by Edward Connery Latham. Copyright © 1916, 1969 by Henry Holt and Co. Copyright

Index of Poets

Anonymous 124
W. H. Auden (1907–73) 3, 110, 134, 190
Patricia Beer (1924–) 9
John Betjeman (1906–84) 45
Elizabeth Bishop (1911–79) 66
Emily Brontë (1818–48) 30
Robert Browning (1812–89) 169
Charles Bukowski (1920–94) 95
Lewis Carroll (1832–98) 148
Raymond Carver (1939–88) 90
Catullus (?84–?54 BC) 105
Charles Causley (1917–) 46, 155
C. P. Cavafy (1863–1933) 151
Geoffrey Chaucer (?1343–1400) 58
Charles Cotton (1630–87) 186
Noël Coward (1899–1973) 22
Abraham Cowley (1618–67) 188
George Crabbe (1754–1832) 141
Keith Douglas (1920–44) 116
John Dryden (1631–1700) 130
William Dunbar (?1456–?1513) 72
Lawrence Durrell (1912–90) 4
T. S. Eliot (1888–1965) 52, 135
William Empson (1906–84) 152
D. J. Enright (1920–) 119
James Fenton (1949–) 111
Robert Frost (1874–1963) 79
John Fuller (1937–) 178
David Gascoyne (1916–) 166
Oliver Goldsmith (?1730–74) 87
Robert Greene (1558–92) 60
Thom Gunn (1929–) 25, 103
Ian Hamilton (1938–) 7
Thomas Hardy (1840–1928) 89, 192
Fay Hart 97
Seamus Heaney (1939–) 82
Michael Hofmann (1957–) 137
Ted Hughes (1930–98) 13
Randall Jarrell (1914–65) 145

Alan Jenkins (1955–) 120
Lionel Johnson (1867–1902) 126
Samuel Johnson (1709–84) 186
Weldon Kees (1914–55) 51
Rudyard Kipling (1865–1936) 164
Etheridge Knight (1931–) 139
Valéry Larbaud (1881–1957) 193
Philip Larkin (1922–85) 61
Edward Lear (1812–88) 132
Robert Lowell (1917–77) 48
Antonio Machado (1875–1939) 143
Louis MacNeice (1907–63) 102, 183
Derek Mahon (1941–) 157
Osip Mandelstam (1891–?1938) 109
Andrew Marvell (1621–78) 16
Edgar Lee Masters (?1868–1950) 65
Charlotte Mew (1869–1928) 53
Robert Mezey (1935–) 5
Edwin Morgan (1920–) 69
Andrew Motion (1952–) 62
Paul Muldoon (1952–) 64
Bernad O'Donoghue (1945–) 56
A. B. (Banjo) Paterson (1864–1961) 162
Harold Pinter (1930–) 8
Sylvia Plath (1932–63) 11
William Plomer (1903–73) 41
Alexander Pope (1688–1744) 36, 131
Winthrop Mackworth Praed (1802–39) 99
John Crowe Ransom (1888—1974) 21
James Reeves (1909–78) 20
Neil Rennie (1948–) 194
Rainer Maria Rilke (1875–1926) 18
E. A. Robinson (1869–1935) 50
Theodore Roethke (1908–63) 136
Stephen Romer (1957–) 153
Christina Rossetti (1830–94) 32
Alan Ross (1922–2001) 107
John Skelton (?1460–1529) 122
Christopher Smart (1722–71) 26
Elizabeth Smart (1913–86) 55
Stevie Smith (1902–71) 44
Bernard Spencer (1909–63) 118
Jonathan Swift (1667–1745) 38
J. M. Synge (1871–1909) 160

Anthony Thwaite (1930–) 114
R. S. Thomas (1913–) 86
César Vallejo (1892–1938) 19
François Villon (1431–after 1463) 34
John Wilmot, Earl of Rochester (1648–80) 128, 150
William Wordsworth (1770–1850) 74
James Wright (1927–80) 10
W. B. Yeats (1865–1939) 80

Index of first lines

A shilling life will give you all the facts 3
A man so various, that he seemed to be 130
After I got religion and steadied down 65
All my favourite characters have been 4
All out-of-doors looked darkly in at him 79
Although I can see him still 80
Ancient person, for whom I 150
And now the house-dog stretched once more 30
'And now to God the Father,' he ends 89
As a white stone draws down the fish 116
As some fond virgin, whom her mother's care 36
At first I thought there was a superfine 50
At first we heard the jingling of her ornaments 118
At the noisy end of the café, head bent 151
Beside a flashing gramophone 178
Brother, today I sit on the brick bench outside the house 19
Cinquevalli is falling, falling 69
Condemn'd to hope's delusive mine 186
Corinna, Pride of Drury Lane 38
Dear Alice! you'll laugh when you know it 99
Do take Muriel out 44
drinking with Norman Mailer 95
For I will consider my Cat Jeoffrey 26
Friedrich, at twenty-two 46
Friend, whose unnatural early death 168
From his armchair in the home counties 153
God! How they plague his life, the three damned sisters 20
Habitué of a small-town club, this man 143
Hard Rock was 'known not to take no shit 139
He had fought for the wrong causes 183
He was found by the Bureau of Statistics to be 190
He would drink by himself 82
Her face like a rain-beaten stone on the day she rolled off 136
Here he is of course. It was his best 103
Here lies David Garrick, describe me, who can 87
Here's the ancient floor 192
Here's Uncle Stan, his hair a comber, slick 155
His stature was not very tall 60
'How pleasant to know Mr Lear!' 132

I can remember, I can remember 22
I deal with farmers, things like dips and feed 61
I love drunks. I always have 97
I painted myself into a corner 120
I sit here doing nothing, alone, worn out by long winter 10
I tell my secret? No indeed, not I 32
I've done what I could. My boys run wild now 7
I walked into the night-club in the morning 45
I was in the Forum once at a loose end 105
I went into a public-'ouse to get a pint o'beer 164
I would like to be that elderly Chinese gentleman 119
I' th' isle of Britain, long since famous grown 128
In good King Charles' golden days 124
In the worst inn's worst room, with mat half-hung 131
In this cold monument lies one 184
It was a dismal and a fearful night 188
It's after closing-time on a winter's night 157
Jill. Fred phoned. He can't make tonight 8
Left by his friend to breakfast alone on the white 134
Let us cease our idle chatter 162
Lang hef I maed of ladyes quhytt 72
Mirry Margaret 122
Miss Helen Slingsby was my maiden aunt 135
Mostly his conversation moved around cricket 107
Moving from Cheer to Joy, from Joy to All 145
My mother writes from Trenton 5
My railwayman father voted 9
Now was ther of that chirche a parissh clerk 58
One night a score of Erris men 160
One particular night 62
Our lives no longer feel ground under them 109
Perfection, of a kind, was what he was after 110
Ripeness is all; her in her cooling planet 152
Robinson at cards at the Algonquin; a thin 51
See with what simplicity 16
She flourished in he 'Twenties, 'hectic' days of Peace 41
Sombre and rich, the skies 126
That man, Prytherch, with the torn cap 86
That morning early I ran through the briars 56
The darkness was a richness in the room 18
The girl who mounted in the omnibus 52
The *Kentish Independent* of 1843 137
The sad seamstress 66
There was a roaring in the wind all night 74

There was such speed in her little body 21
They fled from the boisterous sobbings of Margery Kempe 55
This is winter, this is night, small love 11
Three Summers since I chose a maid 53
Thus by himself compell'd to live each day 141
'Tis no sin for a man to labour in his vocation' 34
Traveller! Cosmopolitan! but now 193
Two minutes long it pitches through some bar 25
Underneath a Mazda bulb sits Coconut Joe 196
What's become of Waring 169
When His Excellency Prince Norodom Chantaraingsey 111
Why Brownlee left, and where he went 64
With a pert moustache and a ready candid smile 102
'You are old, Father William,' the young man said 148
You lashed for release, like a migrant eel in November 13
You read the *New York Times* 48
You don't know what love is Bukowski said 90
You want coins? Roman? Greek? Nice vase? Head of god, goddess? 114